SHAMANISM

SHAMANISM

PIERS VITEBSKY

University of Oklahoma Press

Norman

Shamanism

Oklahoma Paperbacks edition published in the United States of America in 2001 by the University of Oklahoma Press, Norman, Publishing Division of the University, by arrangement with Duncan Baird Publishers

Conceived, created, and designed by Duncan Baird Publishers Sixth Floor, Castle House 75–76 Wells Street London W1T 3QH

First published in the United States of America in 1995 by Little, Brown and Company

Editor: Clifford Bishop
Designer: Gabriella Le Grazie
Picture research: Jan Croot
Calligraphy: Susanne Haines
Cartographic design: Line + Line

ISBN: 0-8061-3328-7

10 9 8 7 6 5 4 3 2 1

Typeset in Times NR MT
Color reproduction by Colourscan, Singapore
Printed in Singapore by Imago Publishing Limited

Contents

Introduction

Each time I return home from fieldwork among communities with shamanic traditions, people ask me the questions: what is a shaman? What does a shaman actually do? What effect is there on the people around them? Yet among the many existing books on shamans, there is little that addresses these questions directly or enables readers to explore the subject for themselves.

This book offers an introduction to the enchanting, but sometimes violent and disturbing world of the shaman. Shamanic motifs, themes and characters appear throughout human history, religion and psychology. The word "shaman" comes from Siberia. There it is pronounced sham-án, with the stress on the last syllable. In English, it is usually pronounced either shár-man or sháy-man: the plural is shamans. The word shaman has been used quite loosely around the world – almost interchangeably with "medicine-man/woman", "sorcerer", "magician" and "witch-doctor", particularly where these figures have operated outside the mainstream of institutionalized religions.

Although I have included other specialists who retain control of their trance, I have focused mainly on the kind of shamans who make a journey of the soul. What these shamans do is so special that they deserve a term to themselves.

The number of people who are fascinated by shamanism is increasing constantly. I have tried to give a comprehensive picture, without mystification, of what shamans do and have done for

The masks on these pages are from a private collection. They are all shamanic masks from near the Arctic Circle.

e (Mörsase) naglimassorssuängormat.
ilíniarfigigâ.

29

A hunter in Greenland is taught the formula for calming the storm. His instructor is a gull. From the collection of the University of Oslo, painted by a Greenlander in the 19th century.

many thousands of years. I have paid attention to their social context because I believe that a shaman's activity has meaning only in relation to other people. Since there are thousands of ethnic groups known to have shamans, I have tended to focus on a number of representative peoples, and developed these throughout the book in order to give the reader a feel for the sights, sounds and odours of their villages and landscapes.

The Shamanic Worldview

Being chosen by spirits, taught by them to
enter trance and to fly with one's soul to
other worlds in the sky or clamber through
dangerous crevasses into the terror of
subterranean worlds; being stripped of one's
flesh, reduced to a skeleton (for a hunting
society, bones are the very core of life), and
then reassembled and reborn; gaining the
power to combat spirits and heal their
victims, to kill enemies and save one's own
people from disease and starvation – these
are features of shamanic religions which
occur in many parts of the world. At the
same time, shamans live ordinary lives,
hunting, cooking, gardening and doing
household chores like everyone else. When
shamans talk of other worlds, they do not
mean that these are disconnected from this
world. Rather, these worlds represent the true
nature of things and the true causes of events
in this world. The understanding is widely
shared in the community, and many people
may be shamans to a greater or lesser degree,
according to their insight into this reality.

*A painting by a former shaman from the Peruvian Amazon. Five
shamans sit around a pot in which they have boiled a psychedelic
plant. Drinking the plant has induced vivid hallucinations.*

What is a shaman?

A photograph of a shaman in a trance, which was taken in Mongolia in 1934.

Shamans are at once doctors, priests, social workers and mystics. They have been called madmen or madwomen, were frequently persecuted throughout history, dismissed in the 1960s as a "desiccated" and "insipid" figment of the anthropologist's imagination, and are now so fashionable that they inspire both intense academic debate and the naming of pop groups. Shamans have probably attracted more diverse and conflicting opinions than any other kind of spiritual specialist. The shaman seems to be all things to all people.

The word "shaman" comes from the language of the Evenk, a small Tungus-speaking group of hunters and reindeer herders in Siberia. It was first used only to designate a religious specialist from this region. By the beginning of the 20th century it was already being applied in North America to a wide range of medicine-men and medicine-women, while some New Age practitioners today use the word widely for persons who are thought to be in any sort of contact with spirits.

The Siberian shaman's soul is said to be able to leave the body and travel to other parts of the cosmos, particularly to an upper world in the sky and a lower world underground. This ability is traditionally found in some parts of the world and not in others and allows us to speak of clearly shamanistic societies and cultures. A broader definition than this would include any kind of person who is in control of his or her state of trance, even if this does not involve a soul journey, as in Korea. In these senses, shamans are quite different from other kinds of spirit medium who are possessed and dominated by spirits as and when the spirits themselves choose and who then need to be exorcized. But even though the shaman enters trance under controlled conditions, his or her "mastery" of the spirits remains highly precarious. The shaman's profession is considered psychically very dangerous and there is a constant risk of insanity or death.

There can be no shaman without a surrounding society and culture. Shamanism is not a single, unified religion but a cross-cultural form of religious sensibility and practice. In all societies known to us today shamanic ideas generally form only one strand among the doctrines and authority structures of other religions, ideologies and practices. There were probably purely shamanist communities in the past but we have only vague ideas about what it must have felt like to live in them. Shamanism is scattered and fragmented and should perhaps not be called an "-ism" at all. There is no doctrine, no world shamanic church, no holy book as a point of reference, no priests with the authority to tell us what is and what is not correct.

Nevertheless, there are astonishing similarities, which are not easy to explain, between shamanic ideas and practices as far apart as the Arctic, Amazonia and Borneo, even though these societies have probably never had any contact with each other. Many current interpretations emphasize the healing side of shamanism, but this is only one aspect of the shaman's work. Among other things, shamanism is a hunter's religion, concerned with the necessity of taking life in order to live oneself. The shamanic view of cosmic equilibrium is founded largely on the idea of paying for the souls of the animals one needs to eat (see pp.30–33), and in many societies the shaman flies to the owner of the the animals in order to negotiate the price.

IN AWE OF THE SPIRITS: TWO FRIGHTENED LITTLE GIRLS

A shaman works in partnership with spirits. In the shamanic experience, feelings of exaltation and joy are experienced only as a counterpart to feelings of fear. A shaman is someone who can handle forces on which ordinary people's lives depend but which also fill them with terror. This sense of awe and helplessness is conveyed in the following account of a Kalaalit (Eskimo) shaman in Greenland who tried to interest two little girls in becoming his pupils. One of them recalled in later years:

"I was shivering with fear. His helping spirits could be heard buzzing and humming from the roof, from the walls and right down from the floor. It was strange, beyond our understanding. 'Now, here comes Amarsinijoq!' he said, and we felt a great commotion in the house. None of us said a word – I was trembling with fear and had a feeling as if my skin was being flayed off me, from my head downwards. 'Now he is in here,' the shaman said. We were unable to utter a word, so frightened were we, nor dared we run away out through that long, dark house."

This monster emerged from an opening in the ice, so terrifying the Canadian Inuit shaman who made this drawing that he failed to secure it as a helping spirit.

Spirits and souls

Human beings constantly modify and investigate their surroundings. At the same time, the physical universe acts upon us, so we are linked to the world in a circuit of activity and feeling. Neither we, as humans, nor our surroundings have full identity or meaning without the other.

This picture of mutual dependency could characterize an avant-garde ecological position, but it is also integral to the shamanic view of the world in which everything – not only animals, but also plants and rocks, wind and rain – may be imbued with spirit. In any system of beliefs, understanding the nature of spirit is a profound theological and psychological problem. In shamanic thinking, "spirit" sometimes seems better translated as the "essence" of a phenomenon – it is what makes an animal an animal, or a tool a tool. Spirit can also be consciousness: creatures, trees, rocks and tools can have consciousness similar to our own human consciousness. At the same time as having their own existence, spirits

The spirits of plants and trees as seen by a former shaman in the Peruvian Amazon.

Two spirits, one of them a dog, that tried to eat the Inuit artist as he slept in a stone shelter.

also sometimes deliberately act upon humans and cause events in our lives. They can love humans, and so nourish us and feel compassion. They also have needs and emotions, such as hunger, jealousy and pride, and so can attack us and eat us or drive us mad.

This kind of religious sensibility represents the fruits of millennia of experience at the same time as it provides a means for acting upon the world. Shamanism is a practical and pragmatic religion, never only a mystical one.

knife cuts while that of a pot contains. Just as every person is unique and yet has something in common, so every stream and every mountain may have a specific spirit with its own name, properties and effects on humans. Spirits may marry humans or endow them with some of their own properties. But with these same properties, they may also overwhelm us. These alternatives reflect the ambiguous properties of the environment itself in which animals, landscape and weather may either nourish or destroy us, according to their mood of the moment.

The consciousness of spirits can merge into human consciousness. The soul of a living human is usually believed to become spirit when it dies, and dead humans may become either ancestor spirits or part of some larger elemental spirit. At the same time, the soul may be an image of the body. The Sora of India see the soul as contained in the blood and so having exactly the same shape as the body it fills. The Sora say that the soul is like a photograph and older generations, like many people the world over, believe that having a photograph taken can weaken a person.

The sense of unity it provides therefore does not deny the distinct identity of separate phenomena. Within the integrated shamanic universe there are many categories. Numerous separate spirits have their own forms, names and qualities. The spirit of the sun is distinguished from the spirit of the moon. Maybe they are brother and sister, or husband and wife. Their resemblance to humans will be emphasized by myths about how they came to be as they are and how they affect our lives.

Bear spirits are big and fierce while mouse spirits are timid but can usefully enter narrow crevices. The spirit of a

An 1890 Cheyenne visionary drawing, from the Buffalo Bill Historical Center in Wyoming, showing a dreamer rising from his body.

Shamanic logic starts from the idea that the soul can leave the body. This happens to everyone at death, but the experience of dreaming is taken to show that the soul can also wander independently and return without causing death. Shamanic societies often see soul flight during trance as a controlled form of dreaming, in which shamans turn an involuntary form of universal human experience into a controlled technique. Many peoples believe that humans have more than one soul. Shamans' souls can travel to other realms, and laypersons' souls may be kidnapped by spirits or enemy shamans while their bodies remain, for the time being, alive. The soul which wanders represents the person's consciousness or personality, while the soul which stays behind keeps the body's metabolism functioning. If the first of these souls does not return, the second soul will not survive long without it. In parts of southeast Asia it is considered dangerous to wake people too suddenly in case their dream soul does not have time to return safely.

However, the anatomy of the psyche can be more complex than this. Eskimo peoples generally believe that there is a third soul, representing the person's name, which is transmitted from one living holder to the next, while the Yuchi and Sioux of North America have four souls each. Other variants are possible: among the Jivaro people of Amazonia the wandering soul is combined with the person's guardian spirit, while among the nearby Yagua a person has two souls while alive and three further ones which become active (and dangerous) only after death. The existence of helper spirits (see pp.66–9, 91–3) suggests that shamanic cultures have an idea of the person which is not as tightly bounded inside the body as is common in industrial societies.

SOUL AND LIVER

Among the Wana of the Celebes, a person's dreaming soul is a small model of that person which resides in the fontanelle; each hand and foot has a "gem" which is also equated with the pulse. Souls can also be represented by the internal organs. The liver can be captured by spirits of the forest, which have the right to devour the liver of someone already fated to die, but do not always wait and can also be incited by a sorcerer. One young man was attacked in the forest, his liver eaten and the wound closed up. He remembered nothing of the incident and went on living normally for a while until he suddenly collapsed and died.

SOUL OF A PERSON AND ESSENCE OF A SPECIES

The Inuit of Canada believed that animals and birds have a group soul. A single word was used to identify all the members of one species. Often, two humans had the same name. This gave them a soul-relationship and a mutual sympathy. So a person's name can link him or her to other people and also to an entire species. In addition, the person is sympathetically linked to dead persons who bear the same name, forming a network of partially shared souls which bridges the living, the dead and the animal kingdom.

An Inuit tupilak, *an effigy brought to life.*

Layers of the cosmos

The shaman's activity is based on ideas of space, and although the everyday world is permeated by spirits there are also other, separate realms to which shamans must travel. If one assumes that spirits exist, and that they exist in a different realm from ours and reach out to affect our health and our food supply, then it follows that when these things are disrupted someone must travel into the realm of the spirits to persuade them to behave differently.

Perhaps "space" can best be understood as a metaphor for the otherness of the spirit realm. If we see spirits as the essence of the things around us, then this realm is not geographically removed. Rather, it occupies the same space as we do but is accessible to only some of us some of the time. This access comes only with great effort and skill. Space is a way of expressing difference and separation, but the shaman's journey expresses the possibility of coming together again.

The gulf in space represents firstly a difference of being. Spirits, whether of dead people whom we have known or of forces of nature, exist not here but somewhere else. This gulf can also sometimes reflect the moral inferiority of humans as they live a degraded existence in a state of separation from the divine. In this light, the shaman's journey resembles the quest in other, more explicitly moralistic religious systems, such as the search for the Holy Grail. It is possible to see this as a quest to

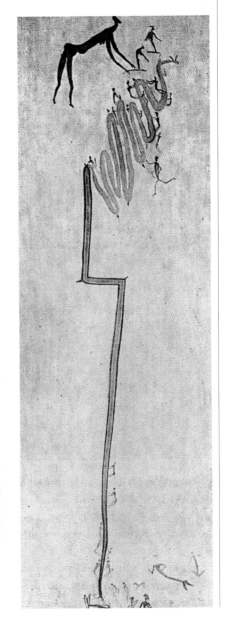

In this southern African rock painting, a tree grows from the body of a woman supposedly sacrificed during a drought. It reaches up to the sky where a spirit pours out rain. The climbing figures are thought to be shamans.

The Amazonian Cosmos

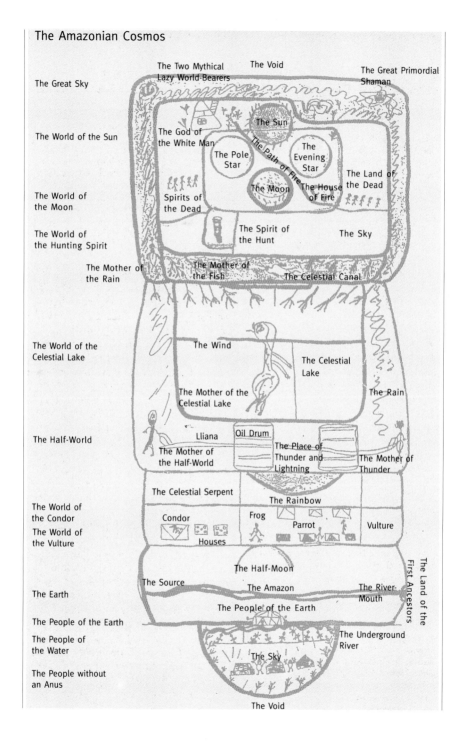

The Void

The Two Mythical Lazy World-Bearers

The Great Primordial Shaman

The Great Sky

The World of the Sun

The God of the White Man

The Sun

The Pole Star

The Evening Star

The Path of Fire

The World of the Moon

The Moon

The House of Fire

The Land of the Dead

Spirits of the Dead

The World of the Hunting Spirit

The Spirit of the Hunt

The Sky

The Mother of the Rain

The Mother of the Fish

The Celestial Canal

The World of the Celestial Lake

The Wind

The Celestial Lake

The Mother of the Celestial Lake

The Rain

The Half-World

Liana

Oil Drum

The Mother of the Half-World

The Place of Thunder and Lightning

The Mother of Thunder

The Celestial Serpent

The Rainbow

The World of the Condor

The World of the Vulture

Condor

Frog

Parrot

Vulture

Houses

The Half-Moon

The Land of the First Ancestors

The Source

The Amazon

The River-Mouth

The Earth

The People of the Earth

The People of the Earth

The Underground River

The People of the Water

The Sky

The People without an Anus

The Void

THE UPPER AND LOWER WORLDS OF THE SIBERIAN SHAMAN

Siberian peoples traditionally believed that the world was divided into three layers. Human beings lived on the middle layer, but the upper world, in the sky, could be reached through a small hole. It had a hard surface with a complete landscape and even animals. This upper world was further subdivided into several levels. Among hunters in the far north there might be only three of these, but in the south under the influence of nearby empires and courts there might be many more and the supreme ruler Bai Ulgen was thought to live on the ninth or even sixteenth level. The lower world was likewise divided into several layers and was often considered the realm of the dead. These other worlds were partly like ours, in that they had rivers, mountains and creatures; and partly different, in that it may have been night there when it was day here. The Nganasan people thought that it was cold in the lower world and dressed the deceased in winter furs. The Yakut, on the contrary, thought that it was cold in the sky, and shamans would sometimes return from a journey to the sky covered in icicles.

ABOVE *At the funeral of a woman whose soul is trapped in the sun, a Sora shaman's assistant fires a succession of arrows to create a ladder. The woman's soul will be led down this ladder to join her dead kinsfolk in the underworld.*

LEFT *In the complex universe drawn here, which is travelled in dreams by a Yagua Indian shaman, the earth runs along the River Amazon. Invisible holes and liana vines form numerous paths between the levels of the universe. The celestial lake is a reservoir which causes the rains down below, and the levels above this lake cannot be reached even by powerful shamans.*

return to some primordial state of grace. The shaman is a specialist in crossing this otherwise impassable gulf, and only a shaman has the necessary technique and the courage to do so.

The separate realm of the spirits need not always be located on other cosmological levels. It is sometimes located on this earth and the shaman's task is to fly to known spots on the familiar landscape. In a particular tribal region in India, one passes the land of the dead on the bus into town. But even on earth, the otherness of the realm is emphasized by the physical inaccessibility or the taboos surrounding the site, which may be an awe-inspiring outcrop of rock or a mountain cave.

The fundamental technique of shamanic travel is a state of controlled trance (see pp.70–73). Shamanic geography can therefore also be seen as a topography of mental states (see pp.154–9). Some psychologists and neo-shamanists today are trying to produce "maps" of mental states, in various literal and symbolic senses. In this, they seem to be following very closely the correspondence which traditional shamans themselves make between their state of mind and their location on a chart of cosmic space.

Levels of reality

In whatever way other people conceive and experience their ordinary surroundings, according to shamanic thinking the dimension of the spirits is permanently present, although it is largely hidden. It is hidden because it expresses not the surface appearance of things but their inner nature. Thus to a shamanic culture there is more to reality, especially to its conscious aspect, than that which meets the eye and the other ordinary senses. One author has written of the Nunamiut, an Eskimo people, that "the spirit of an object may be thought of as the essential existing force of that object. Without a spirit, an object might still occupy space and have weight, but it would have no meaning and no real existence. When an object is invested with an *inua* [soul], it is a part of nature of which we are aware."

There are various ways of expressing the difference between the world of essences and our habitual world of phenomena or impressions. Although they have an underworld, the Sora of India also experience the spirits through a complete overlap between the two worlds, which are frequently at cross-purposes in a way which causes considerable difficulties for the living. The other world is an inversion or parody of this one. The seasons are reversed, and when people cut down trees in the hoeing season to make a clearing for their crops, they annoy the spirits who are already using those same trees as beanpoles to support their own crops, which are just ripening. Similarly, in parts of Indonesia, when the dead speak, although they speak Indonesian, they say each word backwards.

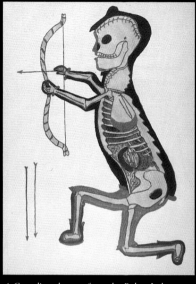

A Canadian shaman from the Baker Lake community pictures himself as a transparent man. Shamans are commonly drawn or painted as skeletons, representing their ritual dismemberment during the process of initiation. In order to heal a patient, a shaman may need to see through the sick person's outer skin to the organs and the bones inside. The shamans of Hudson Bay believe that the inu'sia *– or "appearance as a human being" – resides in a bubble of air in the groin, and that from it comes not just appearance but strength and life. Each species has its own* inu'sia, *and it is this core that makes a man a man, a caribou a caribou or a whale a whale. By thought alone, the Inuit shaman can strip his body so that nothing remains but the bones. He must then name each part of his body and each bone, name by name. In this way he sees himself naked, freed from the perishable and transient flesh and blood, and devotes himself to the work of the shaman through the part of his body which will withstand the action of sun, wind and weather, and exist long after he himself is dead.*

SEEING AND VISION

Among the Inuit people of Alaska, a person who wanted to become a shaman's apprentice might explain, "*Takujumaqama* – I come to you because I desire to see." The idea that wisdom involves some kind of second or inner sight is widespread among shamanic cultures and is often associated with the loss of a person's normal eyesight. In Greek legend Tiresias, who possessed a typically shamanic multiple nature, having been both a man and a woman (see pp.91–3), was struck blind by the Greek Goddess Hera. Zeus compensated for this by giving him the gift of second sight. Other Greek "seers" were also blind, such as Calchas in Homer's poem *The Iliad*. In many parts of the world there is an association

between blindness and musicianship, or the gift of poetry. Homer himself is said to have been blind, and the sightless poet Milton would recite verses as soon as he awoke, which had come to him in his sleep.

Shamanic power is also often expressed in terms of special sight, as when Siberian shamans' eyes are gouged out by spirit-blacksmiths during their initiation and replaced by new, specially adapted eyes which can see other realities. In the photographs below, a shaman of the Hmong people of the mountainous areas of Laos is making a journey into the spirit realm. The metal rings in his hand are the horse that he is riding, and his face is covered so that his inner eyes might be opened and he can see his way in the world of the spirits.

NAMES AND REALITY

The words of Inuit songs are part of the material environment, like snow, bones or skin. They have a functional property, which can be wrapped up, carved and put together, just like the material of any other craft.

I put some words together,
I made a little song.
I took it home one evening,
mysteriously wrapped...

The Inuit believed that uttering a name created a reality, even if only a mental one. Objects and their names were equally real. A person's name is part of their soul in that it symbolizes their social existence and their relationship to the environment. It can also represent a person's essence: it is this which they will pass on to another person after death. Christian Soras say that Jesus is more powerful than the spirits of their shamans, but that they still believe in the old spirits as these have their own names and all names refer to something.

A SHAMAN'S-EYE PHOTOGRAPH OF NON-ORDINARY REALITY?

This unique photograph of Tamu shamans was taken in Nepal at the climax of a rite to soothe the ghost of a person who had died in an unnatural and inauspicious way. The rite is called a *Moshi Tiba*.

Five shamans are sitting side by side and chanting. The shamans and their audience are on tenterhooks, waiting for the souls of the dead person to come (in this region of Nepal, a person is believed to have more than one soul). Everyone's attention is focused on a bird which is tied to a model spirit-house. They are waiting for it to flutter its wings, which indicates that the souls of the deceased have arrived. When one of the shamans saw the photograph he exclaimed, "This is exactly what the god, the witches and the ancestors look like! They don't really look the way you see them in pictures, with faces. These are the exact colours I see, in exactly the right positions. But how can a camera see what only I can see? This is secret knowledge, ordinary people can't see these things. It must be a very good camera."

The shaman explained that the yellow line running right across the picture is what the ancestor spirits who come to protect the shamans look like as they arrive. The orange bar across the shamans' heads is the god Khhlye Sondi Phhresondi who has come to protect them from the souls of witches. These witches, who are actually malevolent living humans, can be seen above the heads of three of the shamans in the form of green wavy lines. The witches are absent at two significant points. These are where the protective orange line is at its strongest, and over the head of one shaman on the right who dropped out for a rest and is therefore not engaged in the spiritual battle. This photograph is published here for the first time, with the permission of the shamans.

The spirit world also contains and expresses the true causes of things that happen in the ordinary world. The two realms are linked in such a way that events in the spirit world have effects in this world, so a successful hunting sea- son or a famine, a healthy community or an epidemic, can all be ascribed to the actions of spirits. When a shaman moves freely between these worlds, this is also a way of saying that he or she can perceive the other reality and under-

stand how it affects this reality. In the speech of shamans and of their societies, these two realities often appear to be merged, so that a shaman may casually mention in the same breath that he took the bus to market and rode a wild animal to the moon. It would perhaps be truer to their understanding not to talk of separate realities. Rather, spirits represent the real essences of things and are the real causes of events in the world of ordinary perception.

Concepts of power

Shamanism involves both understanding the world and acting upon it. The shaman must strive to know how the world functions in order to make the processes that govern life and nature work for the benefit of the commu-

Porcupine quills, which are fired at witches in Nepal.

nity. Spirit is more than just consciousness, and because it is capable of causing things to happen in this world it is a form of power. Much of the shaman's work consists of harnessing it.

The Sora people describe the impulse of spirits as a force, power or energy (*renabti*). Just like the Latin origin of the words "power" and "potential", this word is derived from the verb "to be able". Sora see electricity as operating in the same way as spirit, which is similarly dynamic and capable of storage in containers, transmission along threads, and leaping across gaps. But spirit is far more than electricity, since it is also consciousness. Its impetus cannot be switched off since it has its own will. When shamans negotiate with this power it not only enables them to make things happen, but even to turn into animals.

Since human affairs include much suffering, disease and death this is a dangerous and often dark occupation. Shamanic power is not something to be taken on lightly and often exacts a high price. In Siberia, Mongolia and many other areas, people dread being called by the spirits to become shamans and resist for as long as they have

the strength. Recently, in a remote area of Siberia, the last local shaman died as an old man. He had tried to pass on his secrets to his grandson but the grandson had repeatedly declined the gift, and later explained that he could not face the personal sacrifice which would be required of him, since a shaman's power is fed from the soul-force of his immediate family. His wife and children must therefore suffer poor health and early death as the shaman unintentionally sucks the life out of those with whom he lives.

The spiritual power that emanates from the natural world must operate alongside chiefly power, military power and even purchasing power. Although speakers of different languages may not always use the same words for these, they often perceive analogies between them, and shamanic power has sometimes been very closely associated with political power (see pp.116–9).

Shamanic power depends on keeping control over the trance state. There are many other forms of trance that are not shamanic, such as the trance of mediums in those forms of possession where the spirits are in control of the situation. These are basic to most African

A Siberian amulet made from portions of a bear's kidney, and used for healing.

HOW ANACONDAS ARE NOT SHAMANS BUT HAVE SHAMANIC PROPERTIES

Shamanic ideas are very subtle and our understanding of them is complicated by problems of translation. Mystical power itself is not an easy concept to discuss. The word for a shaman in parts of the Amazon is *payé* and one may be told that someone "is *payé*". One can also be told that the anaconda, as a species, is very *payé* but that the tapir is only a little bit *payé*. Here, the word "*payé*" is used not to describe a role (like "a priest") but as a quality or attribute. *Payé* seems to mean "imbued with shamanic power" and these remarks would be better translated as "the anaconda is a shamanistic animal" and "the tapir is only a little bit shamanistic". The anthropologist who reports this information from the Wayapí adds ironically that it is unfortunate that he is obliged to use a Siberian word to discuss holders of spiritual power in the Amazon, but adds that at least it has left the local expression *payé* undamaged by overuse in English.

In different regions, quartz may be seen as solidified light or living rock. The Huichol call quartz the crystallized souls of dead shamans.

An Arizona desert mesa is often a place where power collects.

FOCUSES OF POWER ON THE LANDSCAPE

A Dakota chief explains power as points of rest or concentration in the movement of spirit:

"Everything as it moves now and then, here and there, makes stops. A bird as it flies stops in one place to make its nest and in another place to rest from its flight. A man when he goes forth stops when he wills. So the god (Wakan) has stopped. The sun, which is so bright and beautiful, is one place where he has stopped.

"The moon, the stars, the wind he has been with. The trees, the animals, are all where he has stopped, and the Indian thinks of these places and sends his prayers to reach where the god has stopped and to win health and a blessing."

Leaves used by the Sora to slap the smallpox spirit.

POWER REGURGITATED FROM THE STOMACH

Power can pass through many objects, substances, forms and actions. Among various peoples of the Peruvian upper Amazon, a shaman keeps one aspect of his power as a thick white phlegm in the upper part of his stomach, which is the most vital part of the body. This phlegm contains spirit helpers which the shaman calls upon for healing, as well as magical darts which he fires into victims to harm them. As the dart seeks its victim and buries itself inside, it is partly an object and partly a living being, partly material and partly spirit. In this region of Peru, in particular, power regularly takes the form of plants (see pp.85–7). The shaman's phlegm is called *yachay*, which is derived from a verb meaning "to know".

A painting of a Peruvian vegetalista *shaman and his phlegm.*

It therefore also represents power as knowledge. The magical substance, the helping spirits and the darts are just three aspects of the same shamanic power, which in turn consists of knowing how the world really is and how to manipulate its processes. The shaman is able to regurgitate some of this phlegm and give it to a pupil to drink, in order to pass on this knowledge and power.

religions, but also occur widely in Christianity and in other world religions, where possession by spirits is generally regarded as improper or unclean, and something to be "treated" either by exorcism or by the casting out of demons. In many parts of the world possession by spirits, as opposed to mastery over them, is particularly common among women. This has been seen as a form of compensation for their social and political powerlessness. For the same reason, possession may be prominent among subordinate classes or ethnic groups. Such an interpretation fits a great many situations, but possession, just like shamanism, is also an

A spirit-medium who is a queen in the Burmese national hierarchy of mediums.

THE RANGE OF SPIRIT-SPECIALISTS IN SHAMANIST SOCIETIES

Shamans usually work in the same community alongside other specialists such as diviners, herbalists, midwives and bone-setters. There can also be more and less powerful shamans. Among the Sora of India, male shamans work mostly in the "lesser" tradition of divining and healing, while funerals are conducted by shamans of the "great" tradition, who are mostly women. Among the Yakut of northeastern Siberia, the "black" and "white" *oyun* (male shaman) and *udaghan* (female shaman) were a wide range of traditional spiritual and medical specialists. Others would include the *otohut* (healer), *iicheen* (wise person), *tüülleekh kihi* (dream interpreter), and *körbüöchhü* (foreteller of the future). The midsummer *issyakh* festival, celebrated by the white shaman, was counterbalanced by an

A carving of wrestlers celebrating the Yakut mid-summer festival, presided over by "white" shamans.

autumn *issyakh* just before the onset of winter, the season of death and starvation. The autumn festival was performed by black shamans, who made blood sacrifices to the evil spirits called *abaahy*. By contrast, with their cult of the celestial gods and their lack of a trance state, the white shamans closely resembled priests.

integral part of the wider culture.

A shaman's power is derived from spirits and can reside in objects, songs or actions, such as the beating of a drum. The nature of this power varies. In Lapland, Saami shamans used their drums directly as divining tools. In many shamanic cultures the rhythmic beating of a drum or some other percussion instrument is an aid in achieving a state of trance. In parts of Amazonia the shamans may swallow spiritually powerful plants and insects as a way of internalizing their power. There are terrible stories of people who have abused hallucinogenic drugs such as *ayahuasca*, which emphasize the dangers of taking these plants when one is inadequately prepared. This is a point made repeatedly by native experts (see pp.85–7). To concentrate only on the chemistry of shamanic plants is to miss the point. Their significance is much wider. Yet spirit power remains elusive and always partly outside the shaman: it is hard to acquire and can easily be lost again.

A graveyard in Port-Au-Prince on All Saints' Day. The voodoo god, or loa, of the graveyard is Guede, who is a favourite of the poor because when he possesses, or "mounts", them he frequently abuses their lords and masters through their mouths, after first announcing "Parlay cheval-ou", or "Tell my horse". The possessed are not held to be responsible for their words while being ridden by the loa.

Regional Traditions

Every landscape has its own spiritual meaning. On the peninsula of Kamchatka, the Siberian sense of landscape sees spirits in the forces of the weather and in the cliffs and lakes of this vast, sparsely populated mountain region. In the lush Amazon jungle, by contrast, spirits are thought to reside in particular species of the huge trees that crowd down to the water. The Amazon river and its tributaries dominate much of South America, and the enormous biological diversity in the waters and the surrounding jungle allows the elaborate use of plant medicines that give Amazonian shamanism its special tone.

Certain patterns of shamanic thought seem to recur across a wide range of landscapes, in many diverse cultures and in many different social and political situations. These may be a survival from the earliest human sense of the divine. As more elaborate societies developed over time, other forms of religion arose and shamanic ideas were often eliminated or incorporated. They sometimes lie hidden within the major world religions.

Wind and snow drive across a winter camp of Koryak people on the peninsula of Kamchatka, in Siberia.

The religion of the stone age

In 1991, the frozen, mummified body of a man was found preserved under a glacier in the Austrian Alps. He was overtaken by a blizzard while crossing a high mountain pass some 5,000 years ago. He may have been a shepherd, but his skin tattoos, a stone disc on a leather thong and some dried medicinal mushrooms in his possession have led to speculation that he could have been a shaman on a ritual or spiritual journey.

Bushman rock paintings from South Africa. Debates still rage over exactly when many of these paintings were executed.

Long before this "Ice Man" was found, the discovery in the early 20th century of prehistoric cave paintings in the south of France had triggered speculation that the half-human, half-animal figures who appear among the ordinary animals may be shamans, and that shamanism may therefore be the original, primordial human religion. In one picture, a man with an erect phallus lies next to a bison, with a bird-headed staff alongside; the man seems to be bird-headed himself and this is thought to be a shaman in trance. This interpretation was popularized in the 1960s by Lommel in a lavishly illustrated and influential book called *Shamanism: the Beginnings of Art*. However, Lommel's approach has been heavily criticized for trying to understand one unknown by means of other unknowns. It uses unproven parallels from societies which are widely separated in space and time, such as today's Australian Aborigines. It is difficult to equate these cultures with the peoples of Europe 40,000 years ago. Although the cultures compared by Lommel are all based on hunting, their local ecological and social conditions must have been very different.

Other writers have recently extended the debate to rock paintings in North America and southern Africa. While speaking of "shamans", they avoid making any claims about these persons' social position or mental health but define their shamans in terms of

Bird-headed human figures painted on rocks in Siberia more than 3,000 years ago.

SIBERIAN ROCK ART FROM PREHISTORIC TIMES TO THE PRESENT DAY

The sheer diversity of prehistoric paintings and carvings from various parts of the world that have been published from the 1960s onward ensures that the possible existence of prehistoric shamans will continue to excite controversy. A major source, still largely unknown in the West, is the Russian study of Siberia and central Asia, a region with one of the strongest shamanic traditions in modern times. While only a few hundred paintings from France have ever been published, some 20,000 have been published from the former Soviet Union. Such figures have been drawn continuously up to the present century, though it would be unwise to assume any continuities of meaning.

Rock art from Siberia, spanning thousands of years, but showing a remarkable continuity of style. The bear-headed figure facing the elk (top right) dates from 4,000–3,000 BC, while the drawings of shamans and their helper spirits (right) are merely some 200–500 years old. The apparently similar figures on the opposite page were executed around 2,000–1,000 BC.

"altered states of consciousness". However, if the social position of a prehistoric shaman is almost impossible to guess, the shaman's state of mind is even more intangible.

The ideas surrounding shamans are so complex and subtle that it takes all the efforts of anthropologists working among living people to discover them, and even then there are many dangers of misunderstanding. It is possible that palaeolithic hunters had shamans in their communities, but the theory cannot be proved. It seems unquestionable that, until the development of agriculture, all human societies were based on hunting and in recent history shamanism has had a particularly strong link with the hunting way of life. This is not, however, a simple and exclusive connection (see pp.30–33).

HUMAN SHAMAN OR SPIRIT MASTER OF THE ANIMALS?

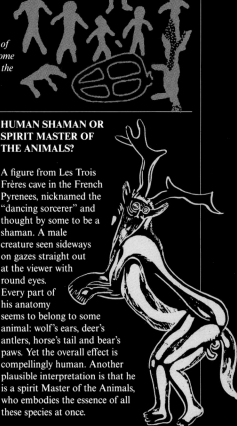

A figure from Les Trois Frères cave in the French Pyrenees, nicknamed the "dancing sorcerer" and thought by some to be a shaman. A male creature seen sideways on gazes straight out at the viewer with round eyes. Every part of his anatomy seems to belong to some animal: wolf's ears, deer's antlers, horse's tail and bear's paws. Yet the overall effect is compellingly human. Another plausible interpretation is that he is a spirit Master of the Animals, who embodies the essence of all these species at once.

Hunters, herders and farmers

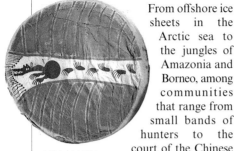

A hide shield from North America.

From offshore ice sheets in the Arctic sea to the jungles of Amazonia and Borneo, among communities that range from small bands of hunters to the court of the Chinese emperor, shamanic ideas have varied much less than other aspects of culture such as language, social structure and political regime, and very close similarities can be seen where it is hard to imagine any direct historical link. Those modern authors who adopt a psychological approach, as well as neo-shamanic practitioners, tend to see the potential for "altered states of consciousness" as being inherently human, which means that these states can be rediscovered in different times and places. If this is true, then the potential for altered states is realized much more in some persons and societies than in others, and takes very different forms in each kind of society.

Even though the existence of palaeolithic shamans cannot be proved, the almost universal association of shamanism with hunting supports the speculation that shamanism may well be the world's oldest religion, spiritual discipline and medical practice. It is even possible that obtaining animals to eat was a more fundamental goal than

healing the sick. This may seem strange today because with our strong contemporary interest in psychology and healing it is these aspects of shamanism that capture our imagination. Moreover, we are now so far from dependence on hunting that we find it hard to imagine the pursuit of animals as being all that stands between us and starvation.

Indeed, some Westerners interested

For the Ainu of Siberia, the bear is lord of the forest. When one is killed in self-defence, or after elaborate ritual, its spirit is appeased by inviting it to a feast and offering it food and vodka.

in shamanism today may be vegetarians, a position which would be impossible to explain to most traditional shamans. The continuity in shamanic thought between human and animal souls is based on the necessity of killing animals. The attitude of hunting societies toward game has been described by one sensitive Western observer as a "complex of worship and brutality". These beliefs tie in with the widespread idea of a guardian Master or Mistress of Animals (see pp.106–9) who is the

keeper of animal species and represents their collective soul or essence. This being releases animals to human hunters in order to provide them with sustenance, but in exchange demands certain sacrifices, and in particular the observance of rules of social morality (see pp.110–15, 125–7). The way in which a shaman's soul flies around the landscape to locate game animals resembles the flight to rescue the captured soul of a patient. Just as living humans hunt animals, so spirits hunt

HUNTERS AND LOVERS

There is a common conceptual link between hunting and seduction, with the penetration of the animal's body analogous to sexual union. Among the Desana of the upper Amazon, the word for "to hunt" also means "to make love to the animals". The prey is courted and sexually excited so that it will draw toward the hunter and allow itself to be shot. The hunter himself must be in a state of sexual tension arrived at through sexual abstinence for at least a day beforehand. He must make himself attractive for the courtship by means of physical cleanliness, ritual purity, magical spells and face paint. If the animal he kills is female, he may express sorrow at having killed "such a pretty beast". In parts of Siberia the shaman, representing the community, may enter into a sexual relationship with the daughter or sister of the Master of the Animals, who is herself a reindeer or elk and represents her species. During rituals representing his marriage to her, the shaman's dance includes wild movements and snortings as

A Huichol shaman is shown appeasing an animal spirit (above), and another beats his "bow drum" with the tip of his hunting arrow (left).

he imitates the male animal in rut. Courtship is one aspect of a wider idea that animals give themselves willingly and "lend" us their meat and skins so long as we show the proper respect to them, to their keeper and to the cosmic and social orders.

human souls, and it is often the abduction or eating of the soul which causes human sickness and death.

Hunting is traditionally a masculine activity, and although the correspondence is not always precise. The gender

An Alaskan arrow-shaft straightener.

of shamans seems to vary strongly with the nature of their society. There are some kinds of female shaman in Siberia, but the classic Siberian idea of the shaman as master of spirits is very much an image of the male hunter or warrior, with his heroic style of journeying across the cosmos and engaging spirits in battle. This type of figure continues into societies such as those of Mongolia and Central Asia, where hunting has gradually been superseded over hundreds or thousands of years by the keeping of large herds of semi-domesticated animals. Female shamans become more prominent in agrarian, crop-growing societies, as is the case in South and Southeast Asia. Sora woman shamans in India sometimes hold a sword or axe as they go into trance in order to fight with neighbouring tribesmen and were-leopards on their soul journey, but in many regions women's imagery tends to be domestic rather than heroic. In Korea, all shamans are women, or occasionally men dressed as women, and the Korean shaman has been called "a woman among women, a ritual expert of and for housewives".

Situations such as these suggest that a concentration on healing represents a reduction in the full scope of shamanism. Wherever hunting and warfare exist in a shamanistic society, shamanism lies at the heart of these activities. Hunting imagery often persists and retains a strong ideological value and emotional charge in societies where hunting has long ceased to be a serious economic activity, or even to be practised at all. At the same time, in herding and crop-growing societies the emphasis of ritual shifts away from the body of the hunted animal, which is always shown respect and may be given an offering of food and alcohol, to that of a domestic animal which is sacrificed.

Shamanism may be a particularly appropriate religion for a classless hunting society, but shamans also function under the most diverse social and political systems. As the importance of hunting declines, other forms of religion, divination and healing begin to appear and the shamanic element which remains in them becomes increasingly ambiguous and hard to pinpoint. The shaman as a single central figure is joined or replaced by a range of complementary and parallel specialists. This process is linked with the growth of the nation state, which can hardly arise on the basis of a pure hunting economy. In societies with a more complex social organization, natural human anxieties about chance and misfortune shift from hunting to floods and crop failure, passports and permits, and passing exams or finding a job.

At a Sora funeral, the shaman offers a buffalo's soul for the deceased to use for ploughing in the underworld. Hunting has largely disappeared, and rituals concentrate on domestic animals.

Siberia and Mongolia

This is the classic shamanic area. The very word "shaman" comes from the language of the Evenk (Tungus), a hunting and reindeer-herding people of the Siberian forests. Although some scholars have argued that the word is actually derived from Sanskrit, the term shamanism could strictly be used to mean only the religions of Siberia and Mongolia. These religions, which traditionally did not have a name, share a layered cosmology with a tree, pillar or mountain linking the different levels. They also involved a belief in the separability of the soul from the body and the magical flight of the shaman's soul to the sky and the underworld. Typically, the shaman is initiated by being tortured and dismembered by spirits and then put back together again. Through much of the area there is a special association between the shaman and the blacksmith.

There are, however, very important local variations. On the Pacific coast facing Alaska, the Chukchi and Siberian Eskimo lived traditionally by

The edge of a reindeer herders' settlement in Siberia, during the summer.

hunting whales, seals and walruses. Many different peoples across thousands of miles of inland forest lived by hunting reindeer and elk, sometimes breeding and herding them in large numbers as well as fishing in the numerous streams and lakes. Further south, as the forest gives way to steppe, hunting societies turned toward pastoralism, with large herds of sheep, goats and even camels.

There were many different kinds of "shaman", even within the same society or encampment. Some were healers, others were finders of game, still others warded off evil spirits or contacted the dead. The idea of the pure or ideal shaman, as posited by Eliade, becomes increasingly difficult to sustain in any survey of this ecologically and socially diverse region. Broadly, there are two different strands that go to make up the overall religious pattern of the region. The strand that has attracted by far the most attention involves the kind of shaman who participates in the immanent forces of the world, whether these are human, animal, or elements such as water and wind. In this kind of shamanism the shaman becomes something other than himself or herself, such as an animal. These kinds of shamans travel to the sky, usually in order to redress an unfavourable situation such as sickness. The other strand is that of clan shamanism, which is concerned with the reproduction of the family. This kind of shamanism is associated with the cult of the sky and of the mountains which lead towards them. These cult sites, made of a cairn of

stones with a vertical pole sticking up out of them, are still popular and are called *oboo* in Mongolia and nearby regions. Shamans of this second kind rarely went into trance and concentrated instead on prayer and sacrifice. Such shamans did not turn into animals or travel to the sky. Among the Buryat and Yakut, the differences correspond to a native classification of shamans into black and white. Broadly speaking, black shamans went into trance and dealt with the spirits of the underworld and disease, while white shamans did not enter trance but invoked blessings for humans and livestock from the spirits and gods of the upper world. These white shamans correspond to what in other parts of the world might be called priests.

When religion is closely tied to ecology, it follows that changes in the environment and way of life must be accompanied by changes in religious structures and behaviour. Among small tribes of reindeer hunters and

A Buryat shaman from Siberia.

GENGHIS KHAN'S STRUGGLE FOR POLITICAL POWER

Many different forms of power are seen as functioning in the same way as a shaman's spiritual power. In the 12th century, aristocratic Mongol warriors made animal sacrifices to the sky in order to ask for heaven's blessings on their military

enterprises. One shaman, who had the power of sitting naked in the middle of a frozen river and melting the ice with his body heat, told the warrior Temujin that the sky god willed Temujin to be master of the world. The shaman gave this warrior the title of Genghis Khan. But Genghis was also able to fall into trance and divine the future for himself without

any help. When the shaman later changed sides and prophesied that Genghis's younger brother would depose him, Genghis had the shaman put to death. The shaman's body lay in a tent for three days and on the third day rose up through the smoke-hole to the sky. No more was heard of him and the political ambitions of his faction were broken.

breeders such as the Evenk and the Yukaghir in central and northeastern Siberia, the shaman was a clan leader and negotiated with the spirits for the souls of animals to be hunted. Towards the northwest, for example among the Nganasan, the shaman had less connection with the clan as this was too dispersed. On the Pacific coast, among the Chukchi and Korya, the clan was weak and families could perform some of their own shamanic rites. Where there were professional shamans, they were relatively unattached to social groups and performed particularly spectacular tricks to retain clients.

The context of shamanism in southern Siberia and Mongolia was very different. Here, sizable herds led to larger communities and a strong clan. In addition, the influence of Buddhism from the Middle Ages onward led to a more

ABOVE *Despite increasing modernization, especially since the fall of the Soviet Union, many Mongolian people still live in* yurts, *or tents.*

A sky-cult site, or oboo, *from Mongolia, showing offerings of bones and cloth.*

BELOW *A number of traditional Mongolian sports and contests, such as wrestling, have survived since the days of Genghis Khan.*

social and political significance was constantly changing. Mongolia was twice subjected to Buddhist missionaries, while the Chinese court shared the cult of the sky with the tribes of the hinterland. The sky is male and the source of good fortune and military success. It is often referred to as a father and the Mongol chief Genghis Khan claimed to be the Son of the Sky. The association of the sky with the male line also led to an emphasis on military fortune. For a shaman to claim to be able to go there by himself was to venture into a politically sensitive area and so this kind of shamanism would tend to be found in small backwaters, such as among a tribe of hunters, rather than in the more central regions of empires. Shamanic traditions have also undergone fierce suppression this century under Communism (see pp.136–7).

Shamanism in this region is closely related to religions and beliefs found in two very different parts of the world. Northern America was probably first peopled from Siberia, by hunters who crossed the Bering Strait when it was a land bridge. The shamanism of the Eskimos of the American north is almost identical to that of the Eskimo and the Chukchi on the Siberian side of the water. The shamanic tradition in Mongolia is close to the pre-Buddhist Tibetan religion of *bon-po* and to various forms of religion that can still be found in Nepal and other parts of South and Southeast Asia.

elaborate cosmology and shamanism was more fully institutionalized. As well as being healers, shamans also often served as sacrificial priests. During important rituals, the shaman's role would be that of escorting the soul of the horse or other sacrificed animal to the next world.

By the 19th and early 20th centuries, when the first field studies were made, these shamanists had become marginal frontier peoples sandwiched between the modern Russian and Chinese empires. In Mongolia and southern Siberia, shamanism was also competing with the Tibetan form of Buddhism, called Lamaism. But Mongolia is unusual among shamanist regions in having early, non-European written sources. *The Secret History of the Mongols* and the works of the Arab traveller Rashid Al-Din show that, while Mongolian shamanism a thousand years ago was in many ways similar to that which is practised today, its

A Mongolian ongon, or receptacle for spirits.

South and East Asia

In religious terms this is the most complex region of the world, the home of the ancient religions of Buddhism, Hinduism, Confucianism, Taoism and Shintoism as well as host to long-established and locally adapted forms of Islam and Christianity. Throughout these diverse and powerful religious traditions run strands of human contact with spirits, many of them probably older than any of these great religions with their written texts and institutionalized structures. Almost everywhere in the region, daily life is coloured by the presence of spirit possession, exorcism, black magic, oracles and prayers involving spirit mediums, holy men, wise women, monks, yogis, seers, diviners and priests. Many of these practices involve trance.

However, in all the confusion it is easy to lose sight of any shamanic elements. Religious specialists like the North American medicine-man would not be called shamans here because the sheer volume of religious activity and the richness of traditions give each kind of specialist a distinct identity and domain of action. In Siberia, most specialists are called "shamans" by outsiders simply because the religion of the region as a whole has been labelled "shamanism", but in local languages the terms are distinct. The "white shamans" of the Yakut and Buryat correspond to figures who further south would be called "priests". In South and East Asia the definition of shamanism is tested to its limits but still varies from place to place with the traditions that have grown up among outsiders for discussing each part of the region. Thus, in Nepal, the term "shaman" is reserved

for people who make soul journeys similar to those found in Siberia and Mongolia, whereas in Korea it is used for female mediums who control their trances but do not make soul journeys.

In Nepal, soul flight is found more among the central Asian peoples of the Himalayas than among the Hindus in the southern plains. Throughout the Hindu-culture area, trance is commonly caused by spirit possession without soul flight. Trance specialists in general are contrasted with the sober priesthood of Brahmins, who receive their vocation by heredity and through the

A Taiwanese shaman prepares to release the illness she has taken from a patient.

painstaking study of holy books. However, there is one form of relationship to the Hindu gods through ecstasy or trance called *bhakti*, which often involves driving metal hooks into the body or walking on red-hot coals. This "way of devotion" is considered by many to be equally valid but distinct from the "way of knowledge" of textual scholars. However, it is not shamanism and does not involve soul flight, which in India is generally found only among marginal tribal people. While Hinduism and Buddhism maintain that

A holy man mortifies the flesh as part of the Hindu Spring Festival.

An old Korean woman is herself inspired to dance by a shaman's performance.

the souls of the dead are soon returned into new living beings, shamanism may well correspond to religious beliefs in which the dead remain in an underworld and use this as a base from which to influence the living.

The ancient shamanistic religion of Tibet, called *bon-po*, has been absorbed into the Tibetan form of Mahayana Buddhism called Lamaism, and is probably the origin of Lamaism's numerous demons and elaborate forms of exorcism. Throughout the Theravada Buddhist countries too, such as Sri Lanka, Burma and Thailand, a contrast exists in principle between the pure and austere doctrine taught by the Buddha and the world of the lay population, whose health, agriculture, love life and even examination results are constantly affected by gods, demons and other spirits. Many Buddhist monks are also intimately involved in sorcery and exorcism.

Shamanic soul flight is found throughout Malaysia, Indonesia and the rest of Southeast Asia, where it functions against a background of

SHAMANS IN HINDU AND TRIBAL INDIA

The complex nature of shamanism in this region is illustrated by the Sora, an aboriginal jungle tribe in Orissa, India. Here there are two kinds of shamans who travel to the underworld during trances.

The "great" shamans, who are mostly women, conduct funerals while the "lesser" shamans, mostly men, perform divinations and cures. During trance the Sora shaman's soul vacates her or his body, which is used by a succession of dead persons to speak and engage the living in dialogues. Each kind of shaman has a different tradition of helper spirits, stretching in an unbroken chain back to an original founder at the beginning of time. The work of the two kinds of shaman intertwines, since it is the funeral which reveals which kind of spirit each dead person has become, while divinations

and cures work out which dead person is attacking the patient and then fends that person off with a sacrificial offering. The funeral shaman has a number of assistants who light funeral pyres, dance, sing and impersonate ancestors in pantomime. All these people can be called *kuran*, the same word as the shamans themselves. This is the opposite situation from the Siberian Yakut (see p.25), where every kind of specialist tends to operate separately and has a separate name. Here, by contrast, the emphasis seems to be on

To a Sora shaman (left), the landscape around her village (above) is a realm of spirits.

what all specialists have in common as they each play their own part in the collective drama of the shamanic rite. Although the Sora live a separate life from their Hindu neighbours, their shamanism reflects a close involvement stretching over thousands of years. Each village has a hereditary earth priest whose performance does not involve trance. This resembles a widespread pattern throughout Hindu India, in which people chosen and possessed by spirits are contrasted with the sober hereditary priesthood of the Brahmins. In addition, Sora shamans acquire their shamanic powers by marrying Hindu spirits in the underworld. These spirits belong to the high castes of warriors and kings who for centuries have wielded political and economic power over the Sora.

Islam and sometimes Christianity. As in India, shamanism is often the religion of earlier, aboriginal tribes such as the Temiar and Batek of Indonesia or the hill tribes of Vietnam. As in Siberia, however, shamanic behaviour is very strongly influenced by its relations with centres of state power, and shamanism seems equally to be a religion of communities, such as the Wana of Indonesia, which are not so much aboriginal as distant from such centres.

In China and Japan, full-scale shamanism with soul flight seems to have been much more common in the past than it is today. Huang-Ti, the Yellow Emperor who is credited with writing a classic work on acupuncture, flew up to heaven on a dragon with seventy of his wives and councillors. This kind of journey symbolized a Chinese emperor's power to rule. The achievement of trance through dancing and transformation into a bird seems similar to Siberian shamanism, except that the predominance in Siberia of male shamans, using the masculine imagery of the hunter, gives way to a strong female tradition. In ancient China, female shamans feature as founders of dynasties. In Japan, shamanistic possession among women has continued to this day but has been diluted by Shintoism, while many women now choose to join new religions such as Dojo, which is based on possession and exorcism. The tendency to female shamanism is greatest in Korea, where all shamans are women apart from a minority of men, who dress as women. Generally, it is probably fair to say that in those parts of eastern Asia where women shamans are more prominent, the soul journey is absent and the definition of people as shamans rests on their control of spirits while in trance.

Sri Lankans walking on a carpet of hot coals.

MORTIFICATION OF THE FLESH

In Sri Lanka, both Hindus and Buddhists practise mortification of the flesh as a form of offering, perhaps because a god has answered their prayer to save their child's life or to get them a good examination grade. They walk on carpets of red-hot coals and pass metal darts called *vels*, "lances", through their cheeks and tongue, or hang suspended from a scaffold by metal hooks in their backs. Participants generally feel no pain. Penitents sometimes enter trance, but this is not shamanism: it is part of a wider pattern of Hinduism and Buddhism.

A fakir pierces his cheeks with vels *and hangs cleansing limes from his body (above), while a man in trance holds the lance of god (left).*

North America

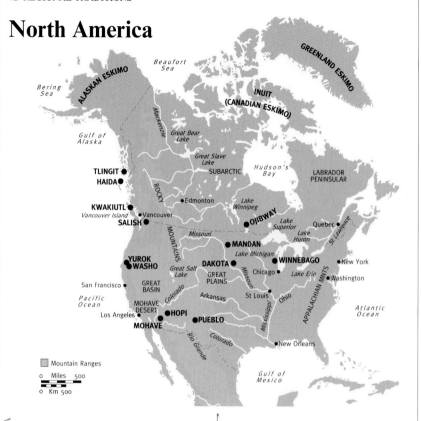

In this region, shamanic soul-flight occurs mainly in the Arctic and sub-Arctic. Among Eskimo peoples, shamans function very much as they do in northern Siberia. For such shamans, dismemberment, dramatic flights through the air and journeys to the bottom of the sea are common. Further down the Northwest Coast, one enters a region which is culturally very varied, in which trance and spirit-journeying ares not universally found. Among various peoples, the shaman may rescue the soul of a patient by travelling along the path of the old ancestors to the land of the dead, making an opening in the surface of the ground, or diving to the sea-bed and returning with blood streaming from the nose and carrying the patient's soul in a little bundle of eagle down. By contrast, in the canoe journey of the Salish, a group of shamans do not enter trance but mime the journey to retrieve their patient's animal guardian-spirit.

Further south, deep trance and soul journey are rare, and the nature of initiation changes. Rather than by undergoing the Siberian experience of involuntary torture and dismemberment by the spirits, shamans often seek initiation deliberately through isolation and fasting. The role of trance and journeying is taken by dreaming or by a "vision quest", especially in the Plains area. Young men, and sometimes women, go into the wilderness and fast for some days to seek a vision from the spirits. This procedure may be followed by all young people as a form of initiation into adulthood. Lame Deer, of the Lakota Sioux, recalls, "All of a sudden ... I heard the cry of an eagle, loud above the voices of many other birds. It seemed to say, 'We have been waiting for you. We knew you would come ... You will have a ghost with you always – another self.'"

The question remains as to whether such people are really shamans. Even in those places where everyone undergoes an initiation and seeks a vision, there are more professional people who develop their visions further, so that

A Blackfoot Plains-Indian medicine-man performing a rite over a dying man, painted by George Catlin in 1832.

The interior of a Mandan sweat-lodge, which was used to induce visions, painted in 1832.

THE SPIRIT CANOE OF THE SALISH SHAMANS

Among the coastal Salish on the border of Washington State and Canada, several shamans join together to form a spirit canoe in order to travel to the underworld and retrieve a patient's animal guardian-spirit. At night, the shamans form two imaginary canoes. Each shaman holds a pole or paddle and the canoe also contains a cedarwood board with paintings of its owner's vision of a spirit canoe. Accompanied by drums, rattles and singing, the shamans' souls sink beneath the earth each in turn singing their own guardian-spirit song. After they have retrieved the patient's guardian, they return it to the patient who then gets up and dances.

The Salish shaman canoe has become widely known through the work of Michael Harner, who has adapted it for use in neo-shamanic workshops. Here, the participants in the workshop form the crew of the canoe while the role of shaman is played by one, trained person who sits inside the canoe next to the patient. The others keep watch around them during the voyage.

SHAMANS AMONG ESKIMO PEOPLES

Eskimo peoples include the Greenlanders and a few villagers in Siberia, but most inhabit the American Arctic. Each of the different Eskimo-speaking peoples has its own name for itself – the main political and linguistic groups are the Kalaalit, the Inuit, the Inupiat and the Yupik – and the word "Eskimo" is now considered insulting among some groups such as the Inuit ("genuine people") of Canada.

Because of this, the term "Inuit" has been used interchangeably with "Eskimo", but this is not really satisfactory because it is not a collective word for all the groups.

The Eskimo are almost entirely a coastal people and their traditional religion is based on fishing and hunting. All became Christian under the influence of early missionaries, although some are abandoning Christianity again as they begin to reassert their traditional belief systems. As the Eskimo's early contact with Europeans grew, they grafted a commercial trapping economy on to the subsistence pattern of their lives. Nevertheless, the elements in the Arctic – especially beyond the northern tree-line – are harsh and the supply of animals uncertain. In winter and spring the traditional Eskimo lifestyle involved hunting whales, seals and walrus. In the summer and autumn they might sometimes move inland, and live off herds of caribou. Everyday rites among a community – which was seldom more than several hundred strong – were generally conducted by laypersons, while shamans specialized in dealing with a crisis, such as starvation. The shaman negotiated with the spirits of non-human life forms such as game animals, the dead, and various monsters.

clear distinctions remain between laypersons and specialists. In terms of healing, there are two main kinds of specialist who deal with two different causes of illness. If the patient is ill because their soul has been kidnapped and taken away by spirits, this produces unconsciousness or some similar serious disturbance and the healer's own soul enters trance in order to set off and retrieve it. But if the illness has been caused by the intrusion of a foreign object sent by a sorcerer, the patient generally suffers physical pain rather than mental disturbance. The healer does not usually enter trance but extracts the object by massage or by sucking, whether directly by mouth or through a special tube made of straw, birdbone or other material. The healer may then display the object to the patient and onlookers. The first kind of healer is a shaman by any definition, while the second is better called a medicine-man or medicine-woman. Sorcery, or black magic, is widely atributed to shamans, and Henry, the last traditional Washo shaman from the California-Nevada border, made a conscious choice to avoid these practices in his own life's work.

North America is the only part of the world, apart from some areas of tropical Asia that were under British colonial influence, for which the very rich ethnography on shamanism is freely available in English. Popular summaries cannot do justice to the many classic anthropological descriptions written around the end of the 19th century, although native religion was widely repressed until at least the mid-20th century. Recently there have been revivals among native peoples as well as movements among urban whites based on their understanding of these traditions and their own needs (see pp.150–53). Native writers and spiritual teachers now often present their own versions of native traditions. Like the accounts by earlier anthropologists, current interpretations of shamanism are inevitably coloured by the preconceptions and agendas of their time.

A bear claw medicine bundle used by a Crow Indian.

THE MIDEWIWIN LODGE

In the Midewiwin ceremony of the Ojibway (shown in a birch-bark drawing, right), a lodge symbolizes the universe, with its four sides representing the cardinal directions. A stone near the eastern entrance represents the permanent presence of the powerful manitou spirit, and a post portrays the cosmic tree breaking through the levels of the cosmos. The state of trance is open to anyone, but a shaman, who must go through eight stages of initiation, becomes particularly powerful – the later stages are considered psychologically dangerous because of the awesome powers contacted. The shaman-initiate lies down and a special kind of shell is placed on various parts of his body in order to localize the manitou there. The shaman-members of the society then symbolically shoot him in these places, while the candidate re-enacts the state of trance of the solitary visionary in the wilderness.

South and Central America

A Kaiapo Indian wearing a necklace of jaguars' claws.

The shaman is a dominant figure in a great many native Central and South American societies. Despite the great distance from the Bering Strait, South American shamanism bears striking similarities to the forms of shamanism in Siberia, from where the native Americans migrated. Cosmologies are often layered, with a world tree or pillar, and shamans fly to upper and lower worlds. Shamanic initiation often involves an initial sickness, the experience of being dismembered or reduced to a skeleton, use of numerous helper spirits and marriage to a spirit spouse. The similarities to Siberia are perhaps the strongest evidence for the basic durability of shamanic ideas over the widest range of environments, social structures and historical periods.

Yet South American shamanism also has some highly distinctive features. Perhaps the most important is the elaborate use of hallucinogenic plants to induce trance and visions. About one hundred plants are used in the Americas, although the range of available psychotropic plants is probably no greater than in the Old World, where they are used much less. Some common hallucinogenic plants, such as *datura* and *peyote*, are also used in southern North America, but it is in South America that the most species are used, and the most intensively. In Central America, the Mazatec use *psilocybe*

HOW SHAMANS TURN INTO JAGUARS

A distinctive feature of Amazonian shamanism is the close identification between the shaman and the jaguar, and in many languages they are called by variants of the same name. Shamans may turn into jaguars by singing spells, putting on jaguar ornaments, teeth and skins, or by taking hallucinogenic drugs. Guahibo shamans keep their hallucinogenic snuff in a hollow jaguar bone with a stopper at each end. Shamans may also become jaguars

for good when they die. Like the Siberian loon, a bird whose form is adopted by shamans, but much more powerful and aggressive, the jaguar is a creature which can move freely on land, above ground and in the water. It climbs huge trees in the manner of a shaman's soul and is also a superb swimmer, so that many peoples believe in water-jaguars which live at the bottom of rivers and who can be reached only by shamans. A Peruvian *vegetalista* may protect himself with a spell:

Where are you coming from,
offspring of the black jaguar?
You nourish the earth with
the milk of your breasts,
In this way you came forth.

HUICHOL
Mexico City
Veracruz
MAZATEC

Lake Nicaragua
CUNA
COSTA RICA
PANAMA
Orinoco ● WARAO
GUYANA SURINAME
COLOMBIA VENEZUELA FRENCH GUIANA
● WAKUÉNAI
● DESANA
● SIONA
ACHUAR ● ● PERUVIAN MESTIZO
JIVARO ● ● YAGUA
SHIPIBO-CONIBO ●
Lima ● PERU ● MATSES
● KAGWAHIV
BRAZIL
CHILE
Rio de Janiero
Santiago ●
Buenos Aires
ARGENTINA

Atlantic Ocean
Pacific Ocean
Negro Amazon
Madeira
Xingu
Araguaia
Tocantins
San Francisco
Paraguay
Paraná
ANDES
ANDES

Mountain Ranges

0   Miles   500
0   Km   500

A yarn painting of a Huichol shaman from Mexico.

Behind it comes,
The jaguar is calling him,
In the midst of the great forest
It comes screaming.
Behind him it comes,
The jaguar already tamed,
My tinguna is likewise,
It comes behind him.

A tinguna is a kind of electromagnetic force-field. Among the Desana, the shaman turns into a jaguar after taking a particularly large dose of snuff. After months of fasting and sleepless nights spent chanting, a group of novices will be called together by their living teacher. It is at this point that the snuff itself "chooses" who is to become a true shaman. One must have courage and determination when taking the snuff. Some novices merely feel violently sick, while others pass on through their headache and dizziness and turn into jaguars. While their bodies lie in their hammocks, their souls soar up to the Milky Way or roam the jungle. These shamans devour their enemies, and even the ordinary jaguars of the jungle become more fierce and dangerous.

If a were-jaguar intends no harm, it may have a black and yellow spotted orchid behind its ear. The jaguar form lasts only as long as the effects of the snuff and afterwards the shaman becomes human again.

LEFT *A young mother wears the facial tattoo and jaguar whiskers of the Matses tribe.*

The dense jungle surrounding the Amazon River provides a wide array of plant medicines.

mushrooms to induce hallucinations, while the Huichol religion is based around the *peyote* cactus, which is "hunted" as if it were a deer. Tobacco, although strictly speaking not hallucinogenic, is widely considered a sacred plant and tobacco smoke is often used in ritual for purification.

The South American shaman is distinguished from the ordinary person through mastery of trance and soul flight. These lead to the acquisition of helper spirits and of songs and chants. Chants are particularly powerful in this region as expressions of the shaman's power and it seems that shamans can sometimes achieve altered states of consciousness through melodies alone. A shaman may lose this power through becoming contaminated, violating a taboo or being attacked by a more powerful shaman. The shaman's power must be constantly cultivated and its loss may lead to illness and perhaps death. Among peoples such as the Matsigenka, Siona, Kagwahiv and Shipibo-Conibo, ordinary peoples are

thought to possess shamanic power, which increases as they grow into adults. Those who go on to train as shamans are those who increase this power to the point where they can use it to intervene in the many processes that are governed by spirits.

There are many kinds of shaman. Among the Wakuenai, owners of chants do not take hallucinogenic plants and are distinguished from those who do. Among the Desana, the shaman who takes hallucinogens turns into a jaguar and is distinguished from the shaman who owns chants and heals by singing the names of plants, animals and spirits, as well as from another kind of shaman who can travel in the aquatic realms of the universe. Shamanism is closely allied to sorcery and often there are no separate terms for the shaman who heals and the shaman who harms. This ambiguity in the shaman may be specially marked in communities where structures of authority are weak or fluid. Where chieftainship is weak, the knowledge brought back by the

RATTLES

While the drum is the instrument of shamanism in Siberia, it is joined in North America by the rattle (right). In South America the rattle takes over almost completely. Just as the Siberian drum is thought to be made from the world tree, so the handle of the South American rattle is held to symbolize this tree, while the hollow gourd of the rattle is often thought to represent the cosmos. The seeds or pebbles inside are spirits and souls of ancestors. Shaking the rattle activates these spirits who will then assist the shaman.

shaman from other worlds is particularly important and authoritative as a source of morality and social control. The quality of being a shaman is not so much a fixed role as an expression of the kind of power which he or she has.

The colonial history of South

America has been very violent and in many ways this violence continues. Shamanic ideas have featured in some social and revolutionary movements. The Wakuenai on the border of Brazil and Venezuela have a long history of belief in Messiahs and during the 19th century the messianic leader Venancio Kamiko used indigenous shamanic imagery to protest at white invasion of Indian territory. Shamanism is not confined to purely Indian communities. The Mestizo shamans in Peru, called *vegetalista* because of their skill with

hallucinogenic plants, are of mixed native and European ancestry and speak Spanish as their mother tongue. They have lost their Indian ethnic identity but continue to practise a form of shamanism which is typical of the upper Amazon region.

The Huichol people of Central Mexico (left) take peyote *cactus to achieve hallucinogenic visions, in which they often see the stories for their brightly coloured yarn paintings. In the example below, a horned shaman rises to the sky world. A wise Huichol ancestor can rejoin the living as a rock crystal, and this ancestral soul may be put into a fermented drink that is consumed by a living shaman.*

The rest of the world

Shamanic motifs occur throughout the world, although usually there are not enough of them in one place to make up an entire shamanic complex. A frequent motif is that of a tree or ladder connecting earth and heaven. The European story of Jack and the beanstalk closely resembles a Yakut shaman's rescue of the woman abducted as a prospective bride by the raven-headed people in the sky (see p.101). The princess is captured and taken to the giant's castle in the clouds; Jack climbs up there, does battle with the giant and saves the princess. The main difference is that, as we now tell it, this story is not the foundation of a society and a system of morality.

Shamanic motifs acquire a moral dimension wherever the emphasis is on the gulf between this world and heaven. The Dinka of southern Sudan, whose religion is in some ways reminiscent of the Old Testament, say that earth and sky were once very close together but that human misdeeds caused the sky to move far away, so that bridging the gap has become a problem. In this light, Christ himself can be seen as a kind of shaman as he travels between heaven and earth in order to bring about the moral salvation of humanity.

In most African cultures, people do not travel to the spirits' world. Instead the spirits come to this world, and trance occurs when people are possessed, rather than when they call the spirits and control them, as in shamanism. However, many people among the Bushmen of the Kalahari are able to climb to the sky, and it is possible that shamanic ideas are more widespread than is generally acknowledged.

Among some Australian Aborigines, a shaman is initiated by spirits, who dismember him. In some areas they kill him, open up his body and place rock crystals and other powerful substances inside. Shamans are also active in the New Guinea Highlands. The Sambia say that weaker shamans can perform healing, divination and sorcery whereas only strong shamans can make soul journeys and perform exorcisms. Here and throughout the Highlands, shamans are closely involved in the constant warfare between communities, and much of their effort is spent trying to kill enemies by magically projecting

Among the Aranta or Arunda people of central Australia, an initiate is beheaded by spirits and carried off to a cave or underground where his body is rebuilt. He returns to his community in a state of temporary madness.

splinters of bone and teeth, as well as undoing the effects of other people's sorcery on their own community.

There are also traces of shamanic themes in the European past. The German god Odin underwent an ordeal of initiation by hanging in the world tree, Yggdrasil. He could also change into various animals and travel to distant places. Related themes occur in

Jacob's Ladder, painted by Sidney Nolan (b.1917). The biblical story emphasizes the gap between heaven and earth. Rungs are widely used in Christian and Islamic mysticism to symbolize the stages of the soul's ascent to God.

Celtic and Norse mythology. But even the religious historian Eliade admits that these do not necessarily add up to entire systems of shamanism. However, the Saami, or Lapps, of northern Scandinavia did have a form of shamanic practice very like that of Siberia until it was repressed by the authorities in the 17th and 18th centuries. The old Saami religion is probably related to their historical connections with tribes further east around the Ural mountains.

Ancient Greek culture contains striking shamanistic elements, and attempts have also been made to trace these to eastern roots, through the Scythian tribes of the Russian and Central Asian steppes. Orpheus, like Hercules, went to the underworld to retrieve the soul of someone who had died young (see pp.99). This type of journey involved typical shamanic themes of overcoming guardians and obstacles, and negotiating with the king of the underworld.

AN AFRICAN BUSHMAN CLIMBS TO THE SKY

The Bushman says: "The giraffe came and took me off again. We came to a river and I swam down it with my head downstream. Then my protector told me that I would be able to cure people by going into trance. We entered the earth and when we emerged we began to climb up a thread to the sky. Up there in the sky the spirits and the dead people sing for me so that I can dance. If a person dies, I carry him on my back, I dance him so that God will give his spirit to me and then I put his spirit back into his body. When you approach God, all sorts of mambas, pythons, bees and locusts bite you. And when you return into your body you go 'He-e-e-e!' This is the sound of you getting back into your body." Ancient bushman rock art, such as the giraffe from the Erongo Mountains (below), may refer to such shamanic experiences.

Becoming a Shaman

The shaman's activities depend closely on the ability to sweep the audience along with the power of his or her performance, which must have its effect both on the audience and on the shaman. Shamans use many props and symbols to represent their psychic experience and to affect the experience of their clients. Magar shamans from Nepal such as those shown here use special costumes, feathers of powerful birds, and drums and bells to create hypnotic musical effects, as well as the poetic language of spells and prayers.

The shaman is chosen by the spirits, and in the central experience of initiation is often symbolically killed by the spirits and reborn. The personality of the shaman is enhanced as a result of the experience, and this is expressed through the acquisition of the spirit helpers who enable the shaman to voyage across the cosmos. Other, hostile, spirits represent the negative side of the client or even of the shaman's own personality. The shaman's "death" may be repeated or echoed on a smaller scale each time the shaman performs.

The Nepalese shaman on the left is passively waiting for the arrival of his ancestral spirit, while the shaman on the right is calling to his own spirit by beating his drum.

Who becomes a shaman?

The shaman is a neurotic and a psychopath; the shaman is the sanest person in society, deeply sensitive to the moods of others; the shaman is a showman, conjuror and charlatan. All of these conflicting characteristics are regularly ascribed to shamans by observers, and all of them involve many assumptions about the shaman's personality and psychology. In view of the arduous nature of the shaman's calling, it is probably true that a distinctive personality is required, but the nature

A female Teleut shaman from Siberia, beating a decorated drum to call her helper spirits.

of this may vary. Siberian cultures demanded great emotional and physical strength and it was sometimes even said that a man who had lost his teeth could no longer be a shaman. Yet a tearful, spindly child among the Sora may have

the ability to see spirits and be earmarked for the calling.

In native Americans, shamanic powers may be spread widely. In parts of Amazonia a large proportion of the male population are shamans, though some may be more powerful than others and initiation often amounts to an essential stage in the development of adult male identity. The North American vision quest often functioned in a similar way, and the Sun Dance was explicitly combined with annual puberty rites.

The shaman's special powers may be inherent in a person from birth, in which case they must be brought to light; or else the person may have a predisposition or potential for shamanship

---

A SIBERIAN SHAMAN PLAYS HIS DRUM

"Putting his head down inside the drum, the shaman starts to sing quietly. He sings slowly and dolefully. He strikes the drum in various places with quiet, spaced-out strokes. One gets the impression that he is calling someone, collecting his helpers and summoning them from a great distance. Sometimes he hits the drum hard and utters a few words. This means that one of his helpers has just arrived. Bit

by bit the song becomes louder and the drumstick strikes more often. This means that all the spirits have heard their master's summons and are coming towards him in a throng. Finally the blows become very powerful and it seems as if the drum will split. The shaman is no longer looking at the inside of the drum but is singing at the top of his voice. Now all the spirits have been gathered up. Without stopping his song, the shaman puts on his breastplate. He stands on the

spot bending down slightly and tapping his foot." The drum responded to the touch of the drumstick with the most diverse sounds, from thunderous beats with the sharp clang of iron to the most delicate rustling, a continuous soft hum, accompanied by a light jingling. The shaman also used the drum as a sounding board to deflect the waves of noise so that in the darkness it seemed as if his voice was moving from one corner to another and from below to above and back again.

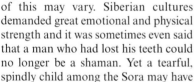

A Nepalese shaman poses with the drum which he uses to call his ancestral spirit.

and must somehow acquire the power. The two states are not always clearly distinguished. The Washo shaman Henry grew up surrounded by two shamans, a brother-in-law and an uncle, both of whom he respected and adored. As a child, he would dream that a bear was looking at him and then he would fly up towards the moon. He was later taken away to a brutal boarding school run by the US Army and designed to de-culture native children, but while sleeping in the dormitory there he received the power dream that set him on his path to becoming a shaman. His spirit helper, Water, was not inherited from his relatives, but the inclination to shamanhood was surely affected by his childhood closeness to them.

In Mongolia and Siberia the element of inheritance is often made explicit, particularly where the male

A Yagua shaman from South America smokes tobacco as part of his preparations for entering trance.

lineage is important. The Mongol shaman had an hereditary right or quality called *udkha* which was traced back to the celestial origin of his line. Tengriin *udkha* was the *udkha* that signified descent from the sky god Tengri, Ner'jeer *udkha* signified descent from an ancestor who was struck by a thunderbolt. The *udkha* was also the mark of shamanism as a profession: blacksmiths had a comparable hereditary *udkha* of their own. In Mongolia, as in some other parts of Asia with a history of states and empires, the hereditary rights of shamans and rulers were transmitted in a similar way. Genghis Khan was conceived when a shaft of light from the sky god entered his mother's tent and impregnated her. He later interpreted this as giving him the right to conquer all the earth, just as his father ruled the sky.

Among the Sora, the main shamans are mostly female. Their power comes partly from the way in which they operate in a society whose lineages are

Two Korean shamans, posing for an ordinary snapshot in between demonstrating their ritual techniques.

male-centred. Like ordinary women, a shaman will marry a man from a different lineage and will bear children to that lineage. But in order to gain her shamanic power she will also marry an underworld spirit, who represents her own brother. He is the spirit son of her predecessor, who is her own aunt. The shaman in turn will bear a spirit son who will marry her successor. While the children she bears in the outside world are lost from her lineage to her husband's lineage, the child she bears to her spirit husband – through an act of symbolic incest – allows her shamanic power to be retained by her own lineage.

The shaman's power may also be bought, as in parts of the upper Amazon. But most traditions emphasize that it is the spirits themselves who choose who is to become a shaman. Henry was chosen, but also paid an older shaman to teach him the techniques that he lacked. Selection by the spirits is crucial. Even with a principle of heredity, a shaman's relatives and descendants will be numerous and it is often not clear who should inherit the gift. The spirits of the previous shaman may wander out of control, as among the Evenk of Siberia, seeking new hosts and causing widespread illness. In many regions the

A LITTLE SORA GIRL'S APPRENTICESHIP

While other people's attention wanders, an apprentice shaman watches her teacher intently during her trance. The future shaman is escorted during her dreams by spirits to the underground land of the dead. The journey is frightening, but the spirits are kind and reassuring. As the dreams become more regular and less disturbing, they lose their fearsome quality. Around puberty, the girl will marry an underworld spirit and begin to develop the ability to visit the underworld at will, by means of trance.

A Sora woman becomes a shaman late in life, because there is no suitable young girl available. The shaman is supported by a bystander.

future shaman may be approached in dreams and visions by spirits who suggest that he or she should take on this role. Commonly, the person falls seriously ill and comes to understand the spirits' intentions during the course of this illness. It may be an illness such as smallpox, which without modern medicine is normally fatal. But for prospective shamans the disease leads to an acceptance of their new role which allows them to be healed and so to heal others.

The Yakut believed that a shaman could cure only those diseases whose spirits had tasted that shaman's flesh during initiation. Throughout Siberia and in many other regions, people may suffer from a quite distinctive "shamanic illness", in which they appear to go out of their minds, babbling gibberish, rushing naked across the landscape with no regard for their own safety, or spending weeks up a tree or lying motionless on the ground. During this period, the people refuse to undertake the onerous life of a shaman and are pursued and tormented by spirits

A Tungus shaman from Siberia.

who are determined to make them capitulate. Almost always, the initiate gives in, but the struggle can be bitter and can last for years. The spirits threaten that if the candidate continues to refuse, he or she will continue to be tortured by them and will eventually be killed. Thus, the shamanic "gift" and the so-called "mastery" of spirits are double-edged: they are not actively sought but are rather imposed against the shaman's will, and as well as granting power also cause lifelong anguish. A similar view prevails in many shamanic cultures.

The imagery of pursuit by the spirits is sometimes sexual. We have seen that the Sora shaman gains her power through an incestuous marriage that takes place in the underworld. One male shaman among the Nanai (or Goldi) on the Siberian-Chinese border was approached during his illness by a very beautiful woman who said, "I am the spirit who has chosen you. I taught your ancestors to be shamans and now I have come to teach you. The old shamans have died and now there is nobody to heal people... I love you and you must be my husband. I shall give you spirit helpers and they will help you to heal... If you don't obey me, too bad for you – I shall kill you". Female Nanai shamans are similarly visited by male spirits. This aspect of the shaman's experience may very well be linked to sexual fantasy and frustration. In several parts of the world, the spirit husbands of female shamans are often said to be lusty, and are able to bring about orgasm in their shaman wives during trances and dreams. Some studies link this phenomenon to the inability of the living husbands to satisfy their women sexually.

In whatever way the shaman is initially selected, he or she will come to fit into an order which is completely different from the order of most other

A Taiwanese shaman called Irubai, outside the home of a patient. In her hands she holds the patient's sickness, which she is about to throw away.

people's everyday life. Just as among the Wayapí people, shamans and certain trees are both *payé*, or imbued with shamanic spirit, so the Guajiro of Amazonia say that a person becoming a shaman becomes *pulasu*, a word which also means "spirit" (unusually for South America, most Guajiro shamans are women). It is not that the shaman actually becomes a spirit, but rather that she joins a range of other phenomena in this world which are also called *pulasu* because they bear witness to the constant hidden presence of the other world. One sign that someone has been chosen by the spirits is that she develops an allergy to the meat of some particular animal which for her is a metamorphosis or messenger of a being in the other world. The way to say "I am allergic to turtle" is "turtle is *pulasu* for me".

DYUKHADE CHOSEN BY THE SPIRITS

Dyukhade, a great shaman during the 1930s among the Nganasan people in northwest Siberia, declared: "I became a shaman even before I saw the light of day. Before she became pregnant, my mother had a dream in which she became the wife of the Smallpox Spirit. She woke and told her family that her future child was to become a shaman through this spirit. When I grew up a little I fell ill for three years. During this illness I was escorted through various dark places where I was thrown now into water, now into fire. At the end of the third year I was dead to the world

and lay motionless for three days. It was only on the third day that I woke up again, when they were getting ready to bury me. During those three days, while the people around thought I was dead, I went through my initiation. I reached the middle of the sea and heard a voice saying, 'You will receive your gift from the Master of the Water. Your shamanic name will be Loon [a diving bird].' I came out of the water and went along the shore. I saw a naked woman lying on her side. This was the Mistress of the Water. I begun to suck her breast. She said, 'So my child has appeared. I'll let him drink his fill, my child has surely come out of great need and exhaustion.' "

Initiation and instruction

For a prospective shaman the initial approach by the spirits must be followed up by a period of instruction. Illness itself becomes a means to learning and understanding, as the future shaman is introduced to helper spirits, shown around the realm of the spirits where he or she will have to operate so decisively, warned of possible enemies and shown the true nature of diseases and misfortunes to be combated.

Especially in Siberia and Mongolia, the first approach by the spirits takes the form of a violent onslaught which leads to what seems like a complete destruction of the future shaman's personality. This is followed by a rebuilding of the shaman, whose new powers are not simply an external adjunct or tool, but amount to a form of insight, a perspective on the nature of the world, and especially on the particular forms of human suffering which he or she has just undergone so intensely. The internalization of all these experiences will lead to the emergence of a new personality, and it is this which is expressed through the destruction of the shaman's previous nature.

The candidate's psychic experience is expressed as a bodily dismantling. He or she may see him- or herself as a skeleton, a theme widely found in Asia and the Americas. In Siberia every bone and muscle is taken apart, counted and put together again, while blood oozes from the joints of the candidate's inert body as it lies in its tent surrounded by anxious relatives. There are other ways in which the shaman can become a changed person, and the terror of the experience can also be tempered with exhilaration and delight.

In this painting by a former shaman, a Peruvian vegetalista is shown being spiritually taken apart by snakes called huatanruna. *The two spirits at the top spin like discs and act as guardians for the shaman's heart.*

One dark night, an Inuit (Canadian Eskimo) woman called Uvavnuk was struck by a meteor in the form of a ball of fire. The fire entered her body and she felt lit up from within by a glowing spirit which was half human and half polar bear. She lost consciousness for a period, and when she recovered she entered her house singing and intoxicated with joy. Subsequently, for much of the time she remained an ordinary person, but whenever she felt the power of the meteor inside her she was able to act as a great shaman.

Initiation need not always be violent. In the North American type of vision quest, an essential rite of passage in the lives of many Plains peoples, a boy typically sets out into the wilderness to fast and pray for a few days in order to acquire a guardian spirit. This spirit, often an animal, endows the boy with its own characteristics, tells him

An Alaskan carving of a shaman's skeleton.

what to put into his medicine bundle, and teaches him medicine songs that allow him to call on the spirit and seek protection in times of danger. The initiation of a shaman does not necessarily involve a single dramatic moment, but can be a cumulative process that lasts throughout a lifetime. The Sora shaman begins her journeys to the underworld during her dreams as a child. The little Sora girl's visits to the underworld are certainly frightening, but there is no devastating dismemberment. As she reaches adolescence, she will marry her spirit husband and some time afterward will

DYUKHADE IS DISMEMBERED AND THEN REBORN

The initiation of the Siberian shaman Dyukhade reveals many of the themes of shamanic death and rebirth. He describes the ordeal in his own words: "The husband of the Mistress of the Water, 'the Great Underground Master', told me that I would have to travel the path of every illness. He gave me a stoat and a mouse as my guides and together with them I continued my journey further into the underworld. My companions led me to a high place where there stood seven tents. 'The people inside these tents are cannibals,' the mouse and stoat warned me. Nevertheless I went into the middle tent, and went crazy on the spot. These were the Smallpox People. They cut out my heart and threw it into a cauldron to boil. Inside this tent I found the Master of my Madness, in another tent I saw the Master of Confusion, in another the Master of Stupidity. I went around all these tents and became acquainted with the paths of various human diseases.

"After this I came to a wide, endless sea. The shore had sparsely growing trees and short grass. There I saw seven flat cliffs. When I went up to one of them it opened wide.

Inside there appeared teeth like bear's teeth and a cavern like a box. 'I am the stone that weighs down the earth,' announced the rock, 'with my weight I hold down the turf of the earth so that the wind does not lift it up.' The second cliff opened wide, saying, 'Let all people, both baptized and unbaptized, take the stone from me and let them use it to smelt iron.' Then one after another all the other cliffs opened wide and each one of them said how it could be used by humanity. For seven days I was held spellbound by these cliffs. It was really they who gave me my instruction.

"Then I went through an opening in another rock. A naked man was sitting there fanning the fire with bellows. Above the fire hung an enormous cauldron as big as half the earth. When he saw me the naked man brought out a pair of tongs the size of a tent and took hold of me. He took my head and cut it off, and then sliced my body into little pieces and put them in the cauldron. There he boiled my body for three years. Then he placed me on an anvil and struck my head with a hammer and dipped it into ice-cold water to temper it. He took the big cauldron my body had been boiled in off the fire and poured its contents into another container. Now all my muscles had been separated from the bones. Here I am start to enter trance. However, she does this sitting alongside an older, practising shaman and it may be some time before any spirit voices speak through her. It would be difficult to determine at what point she has become a fully initiated shaman, and some candidates may not stay the course. One Korean teacher of shamans says that no more than three out of ten candidates succeed in becoming fully-fledged shamans.

The theme of death in the shaman's initiation is completed by a rebirth, and the shaman's movement through cosmic space is sometimes explicitly likened to a return to the womb. As well as being suckled at the breast of a spirit mother, the Siberian shaman was sometimes rocked by the spirits in an iron cradle on a branch of the world tree. Among the Alaskan Eskimo, the underground passage into the igloo clearly symbolizes the vaginal passage into the womb, and the word *ani* means both "to go out of an igloo" and "to be born". While one shaman was waiting between lives to be reborn he felt that the inside of his mother was like a little igloo, but that the exit passage was so small that he would have difficulty getting out. Only when he heard a voice calling him to come out did he finally force his way through the narrow passage. In the same community, a fully initiated shaman who was about to fly out of the igloo during trance was bound with a seal-line, representing the umbilical cord, which ensured that his departure would not be permanent.

It is this imagery which has allowed

---

now, I'm talking to you in an ordinary state of mind and I can't say how many pieces there are in my body. But we shamans have several extra bones and muscles. I turned out to have three such parts, two muscles and one bone. When all my bones had been separated from my flesh, the blacksmith said to me, 'Your marrow has turned into a river,' and inside the hut I really did see a river with my bones floating on it. 'Look, there are your bones floating away!' said the blacksmith, and started to pull them out of the water with his tongs. When all my bones had been pulled out on to the shore the blacksmith put them together, they became covered with flesh and my body took on its previous appearance. The only thing that was still left unattached was my head. It just looked like a bare skull. The blacksmith covered my skull with flesh and joined it on to my torso. I took on my previous human form. Before he let me go the blacksmith pulled out my eyes and put in new ones. He pierced my ears with his iron finger and told me, 'You will be able to hear and understand the speech of plants.' After this I found myself on a mountain and soon woke up in my own tent. Near me sat my worried father and mother."

A painting of the dismemberment of a Siberian Yakut shaman.

The ritual birth of a young woman in Tollo Sera in Nepal. At the actual moment of her spiritual birth, the young woman sits on a platform in a pine tree, which is da suwa, *the Life Tree. She is blindfolded as the ultimate test of her aptitude. The shamans who have accompanied her until now leave her alone, walking away to a large feast at the House of Initiates. If she has not fallen by the time they return, they help her down and question her about her visions.*

some psychoanalysts to interpret shamanic initiation and trance as an infantile regression (see p.141). Clearly, however, not all returns to the womb are regressive, since the shaman re-emerges as an exceptionally powerful and integrated adult. In this respect shamanic initiation resembles the ordinary initiation practised in the puberty rites of many societies, in which every adolescent is said to return to the womb in order to be reborn, this time as a fully-fledged adult, or in other words as a more complete person than before.

Instead of being dismembered, a shaman may also be swallowed by a powerful animal during initiation. In this drawing, a future shaman in Greenland is devoured by a giant polar bear.

Not all initiations are successful, although the social expectations can be so high that a candidate may be embarrassed into lying. A young Winnebago Indian early this century recalled, "They said that if anyone fasted by the black hawk's nest for four nights he would be blessed with victory and the power to cure the sick. So I fasted there. The first night, I wondered when things would happen, but nothing took place. The second night my father came and we sang and prayed together, and I wept as I prayed. Then I passed the third day alone and my father came again in the evening and we prayed again. But still I experienced nothing unusual. On the fourth day I went home and told everyone that I had been blessed and the spirits had told me to eat. But I was not telling the truth. I was hungry and they gave me the food that is carefully prepared for those who have been blessed. All I wanted was to appear big in the eyes of people." Years later he went to a meeting of the *peyote* cult (*peyote* is a hallucinogenic cactus). Here too he failed at first to feel any effect, but eventually, "I looked at the *peyote* and there stood an eagle with outspread wings. The eagle stood looking at me. Then I saw a lion lying down and also looking at me. Then I prayed to Earthmaker and said many things that I would ordinarily never have spoken about." Here at last was the vision he had longed for but had felt inadequate because he had never received it.

A LITTLE SORA GIRL EXPERIENCES HER FIRST TRANCE

The photograph (right) shows the first time Sumbari has sat for a trance. On this occasion a succession of twenty-eight spirits passed through her but did not speak at all. At the same time, however, the spirits that were passing through her father often turned aside to address the silent spirits that were passing through Sumbari. They gave detailed instructions about kinship and social relations in the world of the ancestors, knowledge which will be the foundation of her future practice.

Spirits will start to speak through Sumbari only after a few more years.

Trance and ecstasy

Trembling, shuddering, goose-flesh, swooning, falling to the ground, yawning, lethargy, convulsions, foaming at the mouth, protruding eyes, insensitivity to heat, cold and pain, tics, loud breathing, a glassy stare... These are some of the characteristics of trance. How can these kinds of behaviour be signs of a divine state? Although they are disturbing to many, they are an essential part of much shamanic activity around the world.

The shaman's state of mind during initiation and performances is mysterious. The state of trance seems to involve a focusing of attention in one area accompanied by a reduced awareness of surroundings outside this focus. Modern discussion of trance is often cast in terms of one or more "altered states of consciousness" or even a "shamanic state of consciousness" (see pp.146–9). Some sort of trance is fundamental to both shamanism and possession, but a shaman's trance, unlike

A shaman from South Korea at a funeral. She will chant the story of a journey to the underworld in order to assist the dead man on his own journey.

that of a possessed person, is mostly highly controlled. This is probably due to the nature of the initiation, which is echoed and developed in ritual performances. The little Sora girl, clambering down to the underworld in her dreams, and the prospective Siberian shaman who is abducted, tortured and dismembered in a vision, both repeat part of their initiatory experiences every time they make the journey in the course of their work. During initiation, the future shaman did not yet have the knowledge and resources to withstand the strains of what he or she was undergoing, and the violence of the experience was linked to the shaman's inability to control it. Indeed, it was very similar to involuntary possession. If initiation marked the death of the self, ego or personality, then in regular performances the shaman now operates as a newly formed and greatly enhanced person.

Trance is closely related to ecstasy. These two words are often used indiscriminately, or else trance may be used as a medical term – concerned with a person's physiological state – and ecstasy as a religious term for essentially the same phenomenon. But the American

A Sora shaman enters a state of trance in the company of her assistants. While in the trance she will travel to the underworld to bring back the spirits of the dead.

anthropologist Rouget argues that trance and ecstasy should be distinguished as belonging to quite different kinds of religious sensibility. While ecstasy entails stillness, silence and solitude, trance depends on movement, noise and company. Ecstasy involves sensory deprivation, while trance if anything involves sensory overstimulation.

Rouget contrasts the marabouts, or Muslim holy men, of Senegal, who "seek out ecstasy in the silence, solitude and darkness of their grottos", with the "practitioners of the *ndop*, who enter into trance in the midst of a dense crowd, stimulated by drink, agitated by wild dancing and the din of drums".

Even if we accept this distinction, ecstasy and trance can co-exist in many religions, and even individuals.

A Wana shaman from Indonesia lunges out to catch the soul of a patient.

Shamans may sometimes use contemplation, as in the North American vision quest. Yet the idea of the cosmic journey itself, with its struggle to overcome obstacles and enemies on the way, explains why the shamanic experience tends to be vigorous, especially in the classic shamanism of hunting societies.

AWARENESS OF TWO WORLDS

Reports vary on how far a shaman's experience while in trance is remembered once the shaman has returned to a normal state of consciousness. As early as the 18th century, a Russian traveller was told by a Yakut shaman that he remembered nothing, and other Siberian shamans have said the same this century. On the other hand, an Altai shaman acted as if waking from a deep sleep and announced, "A safe journey! I was well received!" In another account a Selkup shaman picked himself up, smoked, drank tea and then recounted his journey blow by blow. Since trance is a cultural activity carried out in front of an audience, shamans must either dramatize their journey while it is happening or report it afterwards. Shamans can show an awareness of both worlds simultaneously. A Sora woman shaman was in trance when her baby started crying and the person holding it tried to put it to the shaman's breast. The spirit inside her broke off its speech for a moment and said, "No, I'm a male spirit, wait until a female one arrives after me."

A Kung Bushman of the Kalahari in a state of trance, perceived as "boiling energy" or kia.

Helpers and teachers

Shamans cannot function unaided and are dependent for their achievements on helpers, so that their feats are not so much superhuman as super-assisted. Apart from living assistants who prepare equipment and play musical instruments, spirit helpers can range from a single wise ancestor, through serried ranks of spirit soldiers armed for battle, to a hallucinogenic plant.

Spirit helpers may convey the shaman on a journey, like the crew of the Wana shaman's canoe described on pp.71–2. Where the helper is an animal, it may often serve as a vehicle itself by carrying the shaman on its back. Helpers may warn the shaman about obstacles and enemies to be anticipated on the journey and assist in removing or fighting them. Often they provide the shaman with magical abilities or strengths which correspond to their own properties. Tools and weapons may have their own spirits, representing their efficacy. Shamans may also send helpful spirits as emissaries or servants, rather than voyaging themselves on every occasion.

A necklace made of grizzly bear claws, worn by a Fox Indian medicine-man who has had personal experience of the dangerous bear spirit.

Perhaps most importantly, spirit helpers provide a shaman with teaching. They provide instruction in magical techniques and enhance the shaman's perception, while the teaching also represents a process of moral and spiritual growth. It is not simply that an initiate is inexperienced in the techniques of fighting demons, but rather that a young shaman has a limited understanding of how reality operates, an understanding that is still very similar to that of a layperson. All these aspects of development are captured in the Siberian image of the shaman wrapped in swaddling clothes and suspended in an iron cradle on a branch of the world tree, or being breastfed by the Mistress of the realm about which he has to learn.

Helper spirits are often humans, such as an early ancestor or a previous shaman who is now dead. When a Sora shaman enters trance and her own soul departs to the underworld, the voice of her predecessor, the previous shaman of her tradition, appears and promises to lead a succession of other spirits one by one to speak through the shaman's mouth. The shaman's own soul will remain absent throughout the trance and her predecessor will act as mistress of ceremonies. Sora shamans also have another kind of helper, a high-caste

An Alaskan Eskimo shaman's animal helpers surround him during a trance.

The girl Taleelayo (or Takanakapsaluk), drawn here by an Inuit shaman, became a sea-goddess with control of animals after being thrown from her father's boat.

Hindu residing in the underworld. It is through marriage to one of these that the shaman acquires and keeps her powers. These spirits have never been alive in this world but they nevertheless represent "real-life" neighbours.

The boundary between dead and living human teachers need not be strict. Korean novice shamans are instructed by a living "spirit mother" who coaches them through the songs and dances. Among the *vegetalistas* – plant-inspired shamans of Peru – a senior shaman sometimes stands by an apprentice to protect him from evil spirits and sorcerers, as well as to instruct him about rules of procedure and diet. Other anthropomorphic helper spirits among the *vegetalistas* include deceased shamans of other tribes, Spanish, English and Japanese doctors, Hindu holy men and the inhabitants of other solar systems and galaxies.

Many spirit helpers are animals, since these are animate and endowed with useful properties which are not available to humans. A jaguar spirit will make a shaman strong and fierce, and a mouse or weasel spirit will enable the shaman to pass

Inuit shamans are frequently accompanied to the sea bottom by a powerful polar bear spirit, such as this Cape Dorset bear. This enables the shaman to leave his body and fly as the bear seems to when seen gliding through the water.

A shaman from Siberut Island in Indonesia lays out plants and feathers to invoke his helpers.

painters and musicians can be taught their skills by plants.

Whether in those parts of Amazonia where many among the population are shamans, or in Siberia, where shamanism is a rare and powerful vocation, the shaman is a person who possesses extraordinary experiences and powers. The ordeal of initiation leaves the shaman perma-nently changed, and afterward the shaman's powers and experiences become integral to his or her newly rebuilt per-sonality. Having initially caused the shaman's experi-ence, the helper

through tiny holes. Bird and fish spirits enable a shaman to move freely through air and water. Other spirit teachers are plants, especially those with medicinal, poisonous or narcotic properties (see pp.85–7). This is especially common in the upper Amazon. Among the *vegetalistas*, the hallucinogenic *ayahuasca* is itself a doctor, an intelligent being with a strong spirit. The *vegetalistas* also believe that

When an eagle appeared in visions to a Crow medicine-man, its power was secured by tying up its skin in a medicine bundle.

A RIDE ON AN ANT OF KNOWLEDGE

One *vegetalista* under the influence of the hallucinogenic plants *ayahuasca* and *chakruna* was able to communicate in a "visual three-dimensional language" with a large ant, which invited him to ride on its back to its home. This was not an ordinary ant but an "ant of knowledge", and the *vegetalista* later learned that the dust and pollen which cling to a sticky substance coming out of the ant's body eventually turn into the *ayahuasca* vine. As they

A chakruna plant.

climbed a tree the ant explained to its passenger that thousands of years ago the ants were intelligent beings, but that they had degenerated after asteroid collisions destroyed their cities. "The ants became

smaller and smaller and lost all their intellectual qualities and their imagination and became like robots." When the ant brought the shaman home and bade him goodbye, its abdomen opened up and a tiny *chakruna* plant emerged.

Although the boarding-school life of the Washo Henry was designed to regiment his mind and strip away his native culture, he was nevertheless visited by spirits in his dreams.

spirits remain as a distillation and reminder of that experience.

The shaman's identity often seems to merge strangely with that of the spirit helper. Being aided by an animal, or riding on its back, are ways of taking on that animal's properties and involve a degree of thinking and feeling like that animal. At this point the various properties remain external to oneself, but it is only one further step to become the animal and take its properties fully into one's own person.

Yet at the same time helper spirits remain in part external to the shaman, something that he or she must be care-

ful to respect and cultivate because otherwise they could be lost or could become harmful. Thus one of the greatest Sora shamans in living memory is said to have been killed by the spirit of his predecessor and teacher because he made her an offering of stale rice from a previous year's harvest. The Washo shaman Henry was given his power after having a dream in a boarding-school dormitory. He dreamt of a buck, the animal which is "boss of the rain", and because it was raining when he woke up Henry interpreted the dream as meaning that he would be able to control the weather. The first time he tried to do this was to remove some deep snow, but he did not do the job properly and there was heavy flooding. The second time he tried to use his power, he again called down the rain to melt some snow and this time he dropped a medicine bundle into the river. That evening the weather turned warm and it rained. However Henry had used buckskin from his shaman's rattle to tie up the medicine bundle, and had replaced the buckskin on the rattle with thread. The spirit of the buck was offended and Henry lost for ever his power to control the weather.

THE DIVINE INSPIRATION OF POETS

The idea that inspiration beyond a person's normal capacities comes from outside oneself reaches far beyond shamanism. In ancient Greece, poetry, music and the arts were said to be gifts of the Muses, goddesses whose name gives us the word "music". Great poets acknowledged that they were merely channels for the Muses. *The Odyssey*, Homer's epic poem about the travels of the hero Odysseus after the fall of Troy, begins:

Sing in me, Muse, and through me tell the story of that man skilled in all ways of contending, the wanderer, harried for years on end,

after he plundered the stronghold on the proud height of Troy.

This idiom has stayed alive in Europe for thousands of years. Although the Greek gods and spirits had no place in Milton's Puritan theology, they still provided compelling images for his literary vision. *Paradise Lost*, his epic about God's duel with Satan, opens:

Of Man's first disobedience, and the fruit Of that forbidden tree, whose mortal taste Brought death into the world, and all our woe, With loss of Eden, till one greater man Restore us, and regain the blissful seat, Sing, heav'nly Muse...

Voyages to other realms

A Sora shaman fasts on the morning of a journey to the underworld, although she may drink alcohol and smoke tobacco. An assistant lights a lamp which will be kept burning in the darkness below throughout the shaman's journey. The shaman sits down with her eyes closed and her legs stretched out straight in front of her. Then, perhaps beating a steady pulse with a stick or knife, or else swishing grain around with a winnowing fan, she sings a song calling on a succession of former shamans who are now dead. The journey which she is about to undertake is an impossible one for ordinary people, who will eventually make it once only, when they die, and with no hope of returning to their bodies.

The earth and the underworld are linked by a huge tree, down which she must clamber. The path includes dizzying precipices on the descent to the "murky-sun country, cock-crow-light country". In order to make this journey, the shaman's soul "becomes" a monkey, like those of the shamans who have gone before her. After some minutes of singing, her voice peters out and her head flops down on to her breast, meaning that her soul has departed.

Sora shamans make their journeys frequently and calmly. In Siberia, journeys happen much more rarely and tend to be more dramatic as shamans shoot up to the stars or dart between clashing rocks under-

ground. A Yakut shaman in the last century would have gone off alone to meditate deeply. Then, hiccoughing nervously so that his whole body quivered, he would keep his eyes downcast or fixed immovably on the light of a fire. As the fire died down and darkness settled over the *yurt* (tent), he would put on his special voyaging kaftan and take long, deep gulps at his pipe. The hiccoughing would become louder and the shaking more excited as he reached for his drum and drumstick. In Siberia, there were various routes upward. The Khant shaman climbed up a branch which was lowered from the sky, brushing the stars aside with his hand. The Nenets shaman walked up a bridge made of smoke and the Chukchi went up on foot or on a reindeer. As they climbed, shamans sometimes had to hack their way through ice, and large chunks of it were said to fall behind them into the tent. In Siberia, the entrance to the upper world was often through a membrane or small hole, which is consistent with the interpretation of the shaman's voyage as a journey into the womb.

Often shamans use a vehicle such as a bird to fly to the sky and a fish to dive under the water; or they may become the vehicle themselves, in the same way that the Sora shaman can become a monkey. Vehicles express the shaman's extraordinary power of locomotion, which is not available to the unaided human body.

This carving represents the moment when an Eskimo shaman's soul leaves his body.

Shamans sometimes ride in trains or aero-

SHAMAN-VOYAGERS IN LITERATURE

The shamanic journey, with its temptations, obstacles and monsters, is the prototype of many adventure stories in which the struggle to overcome such difficulties is the very mark of the hero. Odysseus, for example, is shipwrecked by the angry god of the sea and sails through clashing rocks and past sirens (shown, right, in *Ulysses and the Sirens*, painted in 1909 by Herbert Draper) whose beautiful singing drives any ordinary man to his death; he is locked up in a cave by a one-eyed giant; and is kept as a sex-slave by a sorceress who turns the rest of his crew into pigs. He also visits the dead in the underworld. Throughout, he is protected by his own cunning and by the goddess Athene, who, significantly, is herself the goddess of shrewdness. The object of his journey is to rescue himself by reaching his wife and home. On this voyage, which is one of self-discovery as well as of the discovery of the world, Odysseus can be seen as both shaman and patient.

A similar combination of adventure with spiritual quest occurs in almost any kind of story which explores conflict and resolution through the unfolding of narrative. In Bunyan's *Pilgrim's Progress*, Pilgrim wades through the Slough of Despond and faces Giant Despair. In Norton Juster's tale *The Phantom Tollbooth*, a bored, spoilt boy is sent on a mysterious journey: with a dog helper he faces a time-wasting demon called the Terrible Trivium while trying to rescue the princesses Rhyme and Reason from Castle in the Air. Initially the boy is a patient but in the course of the book he learns to become his own shaman.

planes, especially when they want to harness the superior technological and even political power of the outside world.

The canoe is used among the Salish of Washington State and is a particularly common vehicle in parts of Indonesia and the Pacific. Among the Wana, the shaman's spirit helpers collect strong vines to tie the boards of their canoe together, then test it to make sure it does not creak. The word used here for "binding" the canoe is the same word used for binding houses and even marriages. The spirit crew's knees bend together as they row in time to chewing betel, a ritually important mixture of mildly narcotic herbs. Point by point, the shaman recounts the slow rise of his canoe to the level of the house porch, through the roof, gradually up to the tops of the trees outside, and on through

A Sora shaman's lamp lights the way in the underworld. The lamp is inherited by the shaman during her initiation.

several layers of clouds. The canoe "sails through the air with flags flying, musical instruments ringing out, birds perched on its railings". On the way, the crew discuss navigation, the lost souls they find and the enemies they face. They cross the boundary between light and dark, dock at a lookout point from which they enumerate all the realms laid out beneath them, and finally reach the realm of Pue, the Lord or Owner, to negotiate for the life and health of their patients. In one performance, the patients were two women and their children, and the fear was that the women's menstrual cloths, which had been hung up to dry and had disappeared, might have blown into a forest clearing which was being burned. Since menstrual blood is the source of human life it must not be destroyed by fire, even accidentally. From the discussion with Pue it emerged that the cloths had not been burned after all, and the shamans' spirits were able to rescue their patients' souls on the return journey and blow them back into their bodies. On other occasions, of course, a patient may be in serious danger and shamans and their

helpers may even be unable to rescue them.

While upward journeys may be frightening but exhilarating, journeys downward tend to be full of menace and lethal obstacles. In many cosmologies, the underworld is the land of the dead, and a shaman's journey there is a kind of death. Although in the underworld, Sora

While a Sora shaman journeys to the shadowy underworld, her lamp is kept alight by her assistant.

shamans must not eat any food that is offered by the dead, or play with the children there, however inviting this may seem. If they succumb to temptation, they will be unable to return. A Sora person who appears to be dying will be urged, "Don't let them feed you, don't swallow it!"

The shaman's psychic journey may also take place entirely on the level of this earth. An example is the Desana shaman in the Amazon who travels to a nearby outcrop of rock to negotiate with the Master of the Animals who inhabits a cave there (see pp.107–8). Another is the Alaskan Eskimo shaman who flew across the Bering Strait to Siberia to see what had happened to a missing person. This spirit journey retraced a voyage which ordinary people commonly made by sea (see p.105). In Nepal, the shaman's spirit travels through a known landscape ranging from the valley of Kathmandu to the snow fields of Tibet. He passes forests, rivers, mountains and cross-

These Siberian Chukchi sketches show a cosmological map for spirit voyages into the sky. Such voyages were often associated with the hallucinogenic mushroom Amanita muscaria.

SHAMANS AND ASTRONAUTS WALK ON THE MOON

Anthropologists have sometimes been asked if it is true that Americans have walked on the moon, but the questioners have then added, "But why did they need so much equipment – our shamans don't need any of that!" For some villagers in Nepal the moon is the land of the dead, and the question arises, "Did they meet our dead up there?" A widespread story in Siberia is that when the US astronaut John Glenn reached the moon he was met and helped by an old white-haired Russian doctor and wise-man called Ivanov, who when he reached the end of his long life had ascended there from earth.

OUT-OF-BODY AND NEAR-DEATH EXPERIENCES

Out-of-body experiences resemble the shamanic journey in some respects. A person may have a sense of floating in the air, looking down at his or her own body and sometimes travelling to other realms and meeting spirits. A near-death experience goes further. Someone who is close to dying may float above his or her body and then drift down a tunnel towards a brilliant white light. The person has a great feeling of bliss, feels impelled to return (but with some reluctance) and then regains consciousness inside his or her body. This kind of experience seems to have become common in hospitals after the introduction of resuscitation machines for victims of serious heart attacks. A person generally has little if any control during these experiences, but they may represent a first step on the path followed by shamans, who likewise cannot control their experiences at first. Some shamans receive their calling only after nearly dying from a serious illness.

Wooden birds used by an Evenk shaman. From left to right, the eagle protects his soul from evil spirits, the raven guards it during trance, the swan carries it to its destination and the woodpecker is a healer of humans and animals.

roads, reciting his movements step by step to his audience. Even his helper spirits are creatures grazing on the surface of the earth. When called by the shaman, they journey across the local countryside along routes which are also recounted in detail. Unlike journeys in the underworld and across the cosmos, such journeys have a particular effect on the patient because the patient's physical and emotional state is mapped on to a landscape which he or she already knows intimately. Sometimes a shaman's voyages take place entirely inside the patient's own body. The symbolic significance of these forms of journey is explored on pp.156–9.

In most of North America and eastern Asia, shamans do not go on voyages when in trance. The Salish shamans present an intriguing compromise: the shamans do not actually enter a state of trance, but instead act out a canoe journey to the land below the earth. One modern cosmopolitan shamanic movement has adopted this technique for use in workshops (see pp.150–153).

Battles with hostile spirits

A shaman from Nepal met a Westerner who remarked how good it must be to live in harmony with the cosmos. The shaman replied, "The main part of my job is killing witches and sorcerers. I am terrified every time before I perform a big ritual because I know that each time, one of us has to die."

Healing the victim of a sorcerer may involve doing battle with the aggressor as well as saving the patient. In addition to darts and harmful objects, sorcerers may send their familiar spirits to attack a victim, or even eat the victim's soul.

Grave dangers come not only from animate, conscious enemies, but also from the fact that a shaman's soul must wander without the protection of its body. The destructive spirits on the way and even the harshness of the terrain, particularly on underworld journeys, symbolize this danger. As the Wana canoe journey shows (see pp.71–2), ideas about the degree of these dangers can vary greatly, and indeed one anthropologist calls it a "slow boat to heaven". In Siberia and Central Asia, by contrast, the sense of danger is very strong. According to a Nenets tradition, it is dangerous to fly near the sun and the moon since they pull you towards them and you may be unable to move away. The man in the moon is a shaman who got stuck there and could not escape. The journey to the lower world, generally associated with the land of the dead, usually involves squeezing through tight, dangerous gaps. The Altai shaman would cross bleak, lifeless steppes towards a dark iron mountain in the distance which propped up the sky. The approach to the mountain was littered with the bones of previous unsuccessful shamans and their horses. The sky banged and flapped constantly against the top of the mountain and it was only at the instant when it rose off the mountain top that the shaman could slip through with one finely judged leap. From here, the shaman would go down through the "jaws of the earth" to an underground sea, straddled by a bridge the width of a single hair. As the shaman teetered across this hair, he could see the bones of previous shamans who had fallen gleaming palely through the gloomy depths. Obstacles such as these are echoed closely in other regions of the world. In Venezuela the Warao shaman also has to pass a pile of the bleached bones of his predecessors before he must enter a hole

A shaman in Greenland is portrayed rescuing a baby that has been kidnapped. His helping spirits are a falcon and a stone-thrower.

A painting by a former shaman of a battle between vegetalistas *in Peru. A healing shaman of the Shipibo people is attacked by a hostile*

Shetebo shaman in the form of a vampire bat. The bat's rays induce lethargy, and must be counteracted with dazzling, luminous rays.

in a huge tree trunk with doors which open and close rapidly.

The inanimate, impersonal nature of the dangers menacing the Altai shaman is itself chilling. But another kind of fear can come from a landscape which is aggressive because it is highly animated. The Warao novice must swing on a vine across an abyss filled with "hungry jaguars, snapping alligators and frenzied sharks", run along a slippery path between demons armed with spears, and pass by a giant shaman-eating hawk. Different traditions speak variously of monsters, cannibals, demons, wild animals, impossible precipices and numerous other ordeals which the shaman must overcome. The Nepalese shaman belongs to one of many traditions in which a shaman whose soul is defeated during a fight with a powerful enemy can quite easily die.

Spirits have consciousness and intelligence on the model of humans, and so can engage a shaman in either a physical battle or a battle of wits. The idea of the battle is borrowed from warfare or from hunting among the living, and the imagery will include blood and gore, or the catching of souls in a trap. The male assistants of a Sora shaman sing at a funeral of how they mount a war party and go to rescue the deceased from a bad place in the cosmos: "Let us hold our axes, let us grab our axes. Let us brandish our swords, let us brandish our knives." In a battle of wits, the shaman must match the cunning of the enemy. In a typically shamanic episode from Greek myth, Oedipus tries to save the city of Thebes from a plague and is confronted on the road by the Sphinx, who asks travellers a riddle and then strangles them when they cannot answer. He answers the riddle so that the Sphinx destroys herself instead and the plague is lifted. A Dolgan shaman in Siberia proved unable to locate the

Shamanic battle themes are carried over into other religions which absorb shamanism. Here, in a Chinese Buddhist parable, Monkey fights a White Bone Demon.

spirit who was making his patient ill, so he invited a singer of heroic epic tales to come to the healing seance. When the singer reached the point in his story where the hero engages an evil spirit in battle and begins to defeat it, the spirit that was afflicting the patient could bear it no longer and emerged from its victim's body in order to help its colleague. At that very moment the shaman engaged it in combat and defeated it.

The shaman may also be subjected to tests in the form of temptations. The hungry Warao initiate must refuse tempting barbecues of boar, tapir and alligator and avoid the sexual blandish-

GOOD AND BAD TRANSPORTED INTO OUTER SPACE

Science fiction "Space Operas" (right), based on journeys through the sky and battles against powerful enemies, serve as a modern continuation of ancient shamanic themes. The film *Star Wars* corresponds closely to a shamanic struggle, with Luke Skywalker as the apprentice shaman, Obi Kenoby as his master, Darth Vadar as lord of the evil realm and Princess Leia (and indeed her whole planet) as the soul to be rescued. The shaman has his assistants, including the friendly spirit Chewbacca, while the hosts of evil spirits are represented by the Empire's stormtroopers. One obstacle after another is placed in the way of the heroes by the forces of evil, only to be removed by the heroic shaman and his team. The powerful weapons used reveal a continuity with shamanism in their blend of ultra-advanced technology and ancient magic.

A SHAMAN'S FIGHT TO THE DEATH WITH THE SMALLPOX SPIRIT

In Siberia, whole clans sometimes perished from smallpox. The Evén believed that the evil spirit of smallpox appeared on the migration routes of reindeer herders in the form of a woman with light hair like that of a Russian. Usually she arrived sitting unnoticed on a sledge at the back of a caravan of visitors. But the shaman saw her and knew that she had come to their place "to pay a social call". The shaman prepared himself for combat. Most shamans were unable to fight alone against the spirit of smallpox, which charged them in the form of a huge red bull. If a shaman was strong enough to win this battle, he saved his kinsfolk; if he lost, all of them including the shaman himself would die, with the exception of two relatives who always remained alive to bury the dead.

A Sora peacock-feather bow, used to sweep away smallpox.

---

ments of seductive spirit women. In other words, the shaman must work out what moral valuation to put on experiences and actions. The buck in the Washo shaman Henry's power dream was standing in the West but looking East. For the Washo, evil souls reside in the East and Henry took this as a message that he should avoid developing the potential for black magic which was a usual part of a shaman's activity.

Just as with helper spirits, so hostile spirits can also be interpreted as corresponding to something inside the shaman's own psyche. The forest, wilderness or underworld are places beyond the civilizing reach of human culture, and perhaps correspond to the "unconscious" mind of psychoanalysis (see p.145). The distinction that exists between good and evil spirits is generally not as clear-cut as in some highly dualistic religions such as Christianity. Like the forces of nature, spir-

A Taiwanese shaman prepares to cleanse a house that is occupied by evil spirits.

Shamans might practise before entering life-or-death battles. Here a doctor of the Sitka Quan Indians of Alaska practises tying up a witch.

its may be either helpful or destructive. The task for a shaman is to enlist their aid, persuade them, and if they insist on working against the shaman, to thwart them. The struggle between benign and hostile spirits reflects the ambivalent nature, not only of the world, but also of the shaman and humanity itself.

Music, dance and words

At the beginning of the Bible God said, "Let there be light," and there was light. In commands, prayers, curses and spells, words make things happen. They create reality by declaring the speaker's intention. "By the power of song we cross this desert," sang an Altai shaman who travelled to the under-world. A shamanic performance pro-vides the language to express otherwise inexpressible psychic states, which can never be described in literal terms, and it may be that shamans are particularly good at fantasizing and at organizing ambiguous impressions into coherent images. The shaman primarily uses nar-rative to organize experiences into an epic series of initiations, journeys and battles. What takes place does not just reflect the shaman's or the patient's cur-rent situation, but is also part of a story. As the narrative unfolds over time it moves from problem to resolution. Obstacles are described only to be removed, and there is a close analogy with psychoanalysis and related "talk-ing cures" (see pp.144–5).

A Korean shaman manifests the Warrior Spirit, and dances joyfully because the spirit has been well entertained. She holds a roll of flags to use in divining, and her chin band is decorated with bank notes which are her divination fees.

An orchestra plays while a Sora shaman nearby descends through the floor to the underworld.

The power of words lies not only in their meaning but in their musical effect. The *vegetalistas* use a range of magical chants called *icaro* which are derived from hallucinogenic plants and also embody the shamans' own powers. Singing, like shamanism itself, is regarded as a culmination of a human's potential for growth: "A man is like a tree. Under the appropriate conditions he grows branches. The branches are the *icaros*."

The experience of the spirit realm in shamanism is closely tied to music. In particular, there is a powerful connec-tion between trance and the rhythmic regularity of percussion instruments. In virtually every region where shamanism is found, the drum is the shamanic

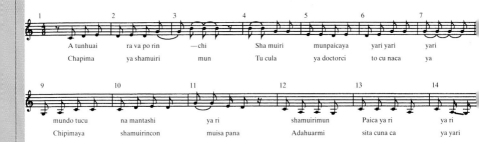

1	2	3	4	5	6	7
A tunhuai	ra va po rin	—chi	Sha muiri	munpaicaya	yari yari	yari
Chapima	ya shamuiri	mun	Tu cula	ya doctorci	to cu naca	ya

9	10	11	12	13	14
mundo tucu	na mantashi	ya ri	shamuirimun	Paica ya ri	ya ri
Chipimaya	shamuirincon	muisa pana	Adahuarmi	sita cuna ca	ya yari

*The great steamboat of the wind is coming.
From the end of the cosmos it comes,
it comes like this.*

*All kinds of mystical healers are coming in it,
also fairies and doctors
from strange space cities.
Strong healers are coming.*

ABOVE *Learning the many possible* icaros *constitutes a large part of the* vegetalista's *training. The chants are learned while swallowing the appropriate plants. The spirit of the bobinanza tree is a beautifully dressed prince, and its* icaro *can win the love of a woman. The spirit of the oje tree creates a fog around an evil shaman so he cannot do harm.*

BELOW *The Tsimshian Indians perform a goat dance to dedicate a new totem pole.*

instrument par excellence. In North and South America the rattle is also widespread, while in parts of South and Southeast Asia shamans may enter trance by rhythmically swishing a handful of rice in a winnowing fan. Sora shamans sometimes tap with a stick on the horns of a beheaded buffalo. The symbolic meanings of an instrument can go far beyond the sound it produces. In the north of Siberia, the drum may represent the wild reindeer from whose skin it was made and the shaman will use it to ride to other worlds. The drum may also be used as a boat or as a container to scoop up spirits, and may be decorated with drawings of animals and of the shaman's family so that they should multiply and be healthy.

Melody can also be important. In the chants of Sora shamans, all melodies are built out of the same pentatonic scale but each category of spirit has its own signature tune which must be sung by the shaman invoking it. After the shaman has gone into trance and the spirits start to speak through her mouth, they sing their replies in their same signature tune and this is a way of

THE PHYSICS OF SHAMANS' DRUMS

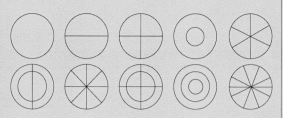

These diagrams show lines of vibration on the surface of a round drum at different frequencies. The pattern of harmonics on a drum membrane is highly complex, especially on shamans' drums which in Lapland and Siberia are oval. Tests on ancient Saami drums from Lapland show that each drum was struck in a limited number of places, presumably corresponding to the sound characteristics of that particular instrument. Saami drums were covered with elaborate drawings of people, animals and the cosmos. Shamans used their drums for divination by studying the movements of a pointer across these drawings while the drum was being played. A typical pointer was a bunch of metal rings called a "frog". The frog's jumps depended on the harmonics of the vibrating skin and modern experiments suggest that these movements are almost impossible to predict reliably.

confirming the identity of the spirit contacted. But the crucial song at a funeral which rescues the deceased by resisting or denying all the categories of spirit which may have captured him or her, is sung in a monotone chant which avoids any hint of melody.

A shaman's relationship with spirits is as much corporeal as spiritual. It is sometimes hard to know where the jerking movements of a shaman in trance, or the acting out of the shaman's adventures, end and a dance begins. The dancing of Siberian shamans imitates the movements of animals and birds, and in general dance expresses whichever qualities are thought to give a shaman power. While Siberian dance emphasizes the relationship with wild animals, the dance of the Korean shaman emphasizes the power gained from royal and bureaucratic spirits as the dancers change their robes to meet whichever spirit or god appears. Here, it is not only the shaman who dances but also the patient and the patient's family and friends. Each one has a personal "Body-Governing God" who possesses that person and dances through their body. For the patient, this dancing is part of the cure while for other participants it brings good fortune. Women find it much easier than men to give themselves over to their Body-Governing God.

Even where shamans themselves do not dance, it can remain central to their work. The *yuruparí* dancing of the Desana is not performed by shamans, but with its phallic flutes and warnings against incest it acts out myths and themes which are fundamental to the cosmology within which the shaman operates. During funerals the Sora shaman sits motionless, surrounded by a small group of the dead person's weeping relatives amid a swirling crowd of dancers, while the spirits speak one by one to them through her mouth. The crowd dances with a movement which echoes the war-dance of the rescuing spirits, as well as the sexual intercourse which will produce a new baby, who will eventually receive the name of the dead person.

Recent interest in "altered states of consciousness" (ASC) has led to theories about the neurophysiological effect of music, especially of drumming. Experimental studies have suggested that drumming harmonizes neural activity in the brain with the vibrational frequency of the sound, but the validity of these experiments has been doubted. Drumming has been central to neo-shamanic movements, where a pulse of approximately 200 beats a minute is said to enable many

The African Bushmen of the Kalahari dance in order to summon up the energy for a healing.

inexperienced people to enter an ASC quite rapidly. The rhythms which produce a trance among shamans, however, are found elsewhere without having any effect. Indeed, when a shaman performs, the other people present hear the same rhythm but do not fall into a trance unless it is expected *Brazilian Xingu flutes transmit the voices of spirits.* of them. Gurung girls in Nepal are said to become possessed when they hear a certain rhythm, even if they hear a recording while abroad. It seems that while music and dance can have powerful effects, they do not so much induce trance as organize it in relation to a belief system. Listeners must also make their own psychic contribution.

DYUKHADE RECEIVES HIS DRUM FROM THE COSMIC TREE

The Siberian shaman, Dyukhade, describes how he acquired his drum: "Then the spirits led me to a young larch tree which was so high that it reached right up to the sky. I heard voices saying, 'It is ordained that you should have a drum made from a branch of this tree.' And I noticed that I seemed to be flying along with the birds of the lake. As soon as I started leaving the ground, the Master of the Tree shouted to me, 'My branch has broken off and is falling... Take it and make a drum from it and it will serve you for the rest of your life.' And I saw the branch falling and actually caught it on the wing."

In this picture from Nepal, a Magar shaman enacts a remarkably similar ritual to that of Dyukhade. Using his drum to catch a branch thrown down from the Life Tree by another shaman makes him a teacher and guardian.

Costumes and equipment

A shaman's costume helps to underscore the expressive work that is begun by dance and gesture. One can move from acting as an animal to dressing up as that animal, or from pulling a grotesque face to putting on a mask. Musical instruments are objects or even animals in their own right as well as makers of sounds: the Siberian drum is also a reindeer or a horse to be ridden, while the Amazonian flute is also a penis.

A medicine rattle from northwest America.

Shamans use many such objects, which they see as a concentration of power in the world. Rocks are often thought to be containers for spirits, perhaps because of their durability, and shamans sometimes keep special small stones. Crystals are used by shamans from America to Borneo and may be thought of as the crystallized tears or semen of sky spirits. Parts of plants and animals are also widely used. Like helper spirits, they endow the shaman with something of their own properties, and may perform actions on the shaman's behalf.

A shaman's equipment is an extension not only of the shaman's person but in particular of his or her capacity to act. The carved, weasel-like Alaskan *kikituk*, like the reindeer and the birds on a Siberian shaman's costume, summarizes certain powers in its owner's mind and communicates these to the audience. Such objects also allow the shaman to perform an associated action. A *kikituk* enabled the Alaskan shaman Asatchaq to heal patients by biting the disease spirit inside them, or to bite an enemy to death. The reindeer on his costume acted as the mount of a Siberian shaman when he wished to ride to the sky. A multiple significance

A Haida shaman's necklace (above) and the moon-faced chest of a Tsimshian shaman (below), both from northwestern America.

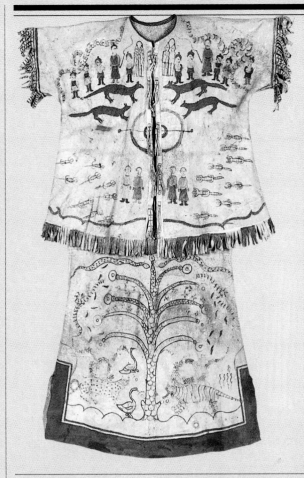

A Siberian shaman's costume, such as a coat from the Goldi tribe (left), represents the mysteries experienced by the shaman, and is the dwelling place of the spirits. The first question one hears when there is a rumour that a new shaman has appeared is, "Yes, but has he got the costume?" Like the gift of shamanizing itself, the shaman may inherit the costume, or he may have it made. One Siberian shaman's costume was destroyed by the authorities in the 1950s and he secretly had another made which he bequeathed to his daughter. She became a surgeon, and it is widely thought that the costume gave her the power to follow a politically acceptable career in healing.

ASATCHAQ'S POWER - OBJECT COMES TO LIFE

Among the Alaskan Eskimo, shamans kept an effigy of an animal such as an ermine or weasel as a power-object. This effigy was called a *kikituk* and was carved out of wood or ivory. The shaman could carry it in his parka or inside his body, where it would enter or leave through his mouth or armpit. He could heal patients by using it to bite the spirits attacking them, but could also send it

to kill an enemy by burrowing into his body to the heart. In one account, a shaman called Asatchaq used his *kikituk* to kill an enemy and then retrieved it from the corpse by gently calling it back. Like the small lithe animal it was,

A kikituk *carved from whale-bone.*

the *kikituk* began to peep out through the corpse's mouth, under the arms and through the ribs. Several times it appeared and disappeared before Asatchaq caught it in his parka and swallowed it.

applies to a whole range of power objects, whether they are birds' feathers tied to a drum, herbs in a medicine bundle, or a dried bear's paw kept in the shaman's pocket.

Not all pieces of equipment are museum-quality artefacts. A Korean living room before a shamanic session is like the dressing room for a pantomime. The shaman arrives with a suitcase bulging with tinselly costumes.

These robes and crowns are bought at a special shaman's equipment shop which can be telephoned in the middle of a ritual if the spirits demand something extra, underlining how a shaman's equipment is partly "real" and partly theatrical (see pp.88–90).

Shamans' rattles are often shaped like animals, such as the fish (above left) and the crane (right).

BLACKSMITHS

In Siberia and Mongolia, the blacksmith was generally more powerful than the shaman. He had a similar mastery of esoteric techniques, but a greater mastery of fire, and he made the metal ornaments which were essential attachments to the shaman's costume (left). He was also the master of the shaman's initiation, as is shown in the story of the blacksmith who tempered Dyukhade (see pp.60–61). Smiths and shamans were nurtured in the same nest, but the smith was the shaman's elder brother. He had no fear of spirits and the shaman, being the smith's junior, could not cause his death because the smith's soul was protected by fire.

A Siberian earthenware metal-pourer used in the manufacture of shamanic ornaments.

Shamanic botany: hallucinogens

Peyote cactus.

Hallucinogenic plants show beyond doubt that there can be a physiological basis for shamanic states of conscious-ness. Yet as with drumming and dancing (or fasting or deprivation of sleep), the cause itself does not explain the content and the emotional tone of the shamanic states. Although psychotropic plants are found throughout much of the world, their use is most highly developed in the New World and especially in South America.

To shamans, the plants are actually spirit teachers and by ingesting them the shamans take the spirits' properties into them-selves. What the plants reveal is not a deviation from reality but a true reality which in an ordinary state of consciousness remains hidden. The Desana are unable to approach any other spirits, such as the Master of the Animals, without first going through the spirit Viho-Mahse, who is the Master of the *viho* plant. In other words, it is the tak-ing of *viho* which gives access to the world of spirits. The drug-revealed reality is a shared, social reality. Drug taking is not part of an alienated rejection of society, as it so often can

be, but a means to a fuller integration of the individ-ual with others. So while some Indian groups in Colombia reserve *ebene* snuff exclusively for shamans, among the Yanomamo on the Brazil-Venezuela bor-der all men and boys above the age of puberty take *ebene* regularly, and its use is effectively a form of initiation.

Non-shamans often take a drug along with the shaman, just as when the Huichol shaman tells his lay companions, "Eat peyote so that you will learn what it is to be Huichol". In curing sessions the patient and the patient's rel-atives may take the drug, and it is possible to say that both the patient and the doctor take the medicine, giving them a shared field of visions within which they can operate together. Sometimes a cure is based on the shaman's interpre-tation of a vision experienced by the patient, who may under the influence of the drug become introspective and

Yanomamo shamans inhaling ebene *snuff to contact a demon.*

*Fly agaric (*Amanita muscaria*), taken by shamans in parts of Siberia.*

Among several South American tribes an altar of peyote ash is made in the shape of a bird to represent the shaman's spirit soaring to the sky.

A Yanomamo shaman.

Matses shamans blow large quantities of ebene *snuff into each other's noses in order to become jaguars.*

review critically the whole course of his or her own life and social relationships.

As there are both friendly and hostile spirits, so one can receive either benign or terrifying visions. Although native users insist that these visions come from the spirits, for those who believe in the unconscious they are open to the same interpretation as the spirits themselves, namely that the source of the vision lies within and that what one gets out of a vision depends on what one brings to it. A native viewpoint might phrase this in terms of respect, and native experts are constantly emphasizing how dangerous it is to misuse powerful drugs. A young man who had a "weak soul" took the hallucinogenic *ayahuasca* greedily and without thought for the people who were to share the brew with him. Soon after, he saw everyone around

Ipomoea *flowers come in both mild and powerful varieties, and may be shared by Mexican shamans and their patients.*

him begin to sprout horns and tails, and then a huge doctor appeared and told him, "You will be able to travel under the earth and through air and water if you go to the pregnant woman sleeping inside that house, kill her with a machete, take out the baby, break open its head and suck out its brain." The young man did what the spirit suggested. Amid the screams, someone sent for the police and the entire group was later given long jail sentences.

As a historian of religions, Eliade saw the use of hallucinogens as a comparatively recent degeneration of "pure" shamanism, in which people achieve visions spontaneously. But even his pure religious experiences are often reached via extreme fatigue, fasting or stress and are similar to those reached under the influence of hallucinogenic plants. Although palaeolithic states of mind are a mystery, archaeologists have found snuff-inhaling tubes and other equipment which show that the use of hallucinogenic plants in the Americas is very ancient. La Barre has even argued that religion itself arose from the visions of ancient shamans and that shamans, as "impresarios of the gods", existed before the gods (see pp.132–5), who are no more than shamans who have grown great after their deaths.

Stirring ayahuasca *(*Banisteriopsis caapi*) in a pot. The plant, whose name means "vine of the dead" in Quechua, is cut into segments, pounded with a rock and brought nearly to the boil. Other hallucinogenic plants may later be added to the mixture.*

THE MUSHROOM'S DEADLY VERDICT

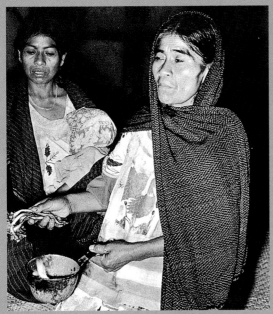

Maria, a Mazatec shaman, holding psilocybe *mushrooms.*

Among the Mazatec of Mexico, *psilocybe* mushrooms are collected in the forest, carefully prepared and swallowed by both shaman and patient. Although the drug is shared, the interpretation of the session rests with the shaman. There is a very moving account of a seriously ill young boy who comes for diagnosis. The shaman Maria, the boy and the bystanders take mushrooms, and the session begins. Maria speaks sometimes in her own persona, addressing the patient and bystanders, or asking a question of the mushrooms. At other times she speaks with the voice of the mushrooms themselves, which are also identified with

Christ because they sprouted from the ground where Jesus dropped his blood or saliva.

Early on, when the boy asks, "Am I all right?" Maria replies, "You are in a tough spot," to which he answers, "I believe so." As the session proceeds, the diagnosis starts to tighten around him. At first, Maria speaks words of comfort in her own voice but as the mushrooms take effect she speaks more and more in their voice, saying, "He hasn't got an ordinary sickness. Now our son has died because a puma has eaten him up, it has eaten up his animal double, the puma has eaten him up." A person's animal double is at the same time both an ordinary, real animal and a

kind of external soul of that person. The two lead parallel lives, and when one dies, the other cannot live. This message is reinforced at various points, until finally the boy realizes the full import of what is being said. There is no hope for him. His animal double has been eaten up and cannot be retrieved, and so he must die: "There's no cure now," says Maria. Bystanders urge the boy to fight death, but:

Maria: It's a holy man, the mushroom says, it's a holy woman, the mushroom says, it's true, the mushroom says, the thing is true, the mushroom says.
Bystander: [to sick boy, but without conviction] Nothing will happen to you.
Maria: A woman who waits am I, a woman who tries am I, the mushroom says, Jesus Christ says so.
Sick boy: Then the thing is true?
Maria: Yes, Jesus says so.
Sick boy: Yes, ai! [he turns pale and collapses, then later:] What will happen? Is there no medicine that my vision will give me a bit of?

The boy died weeks later.

A shaman in the throes of a psilocybe *vision.*

Tricks of the trade

"When the great Khan is seated in his high hall at his table, and the cups are a good ten paces distant from the table and full of wine and milk and other pleasant drinks, these *bakshi* contrive by their enchantment to make the full cups rise up out of their own accord and come to the Great Khan without anyone touching them." In this account from the 13th century, Marco Polo says that shamans could also raise storms like the shamans in Nepal today who lift one finger to make the snow fall and the other to make it stop, or who can turn back a bolt of lightning even after it has set a house ablaze.

Sceptics have long maintained that shamans rely on conjuring tricks. Certainly, some shamans use spectacular effects some of the time, but they claim that their tricks, like their equipment, are not the main point. "I use my rattle and feathers," said the Washo shaman, Henry, "only to gain the attention of the sick person, nothing more." The point of such tricks is to make others aware, through an outward expression, of the shaman's inner power. Yakut shamans often used to twist their heads off and put them on a shelf, from where the head would continue talking. The detachment of the shaman's head was a powerful reminder of a central moment in the shaman's original initiation when the spirits removed his head in just this way. On the first occasion the shaman was passive and helpless, whereas now he can repeat the experience at will and under his full control.

Being a trickster is an essential strand in the make-up of a shaman, who must change form to fight and outwit obstructive spirits. Primeval shamans used trickery to capture the sun so as to give people daylight, or stole the secrets of fire, hunting or agriculture from jealous spirits. A Nepalese shaman in this century was imprisoned by the authorities but walked out through the main gate unnoticed in the form of a sheep. Sometimes, shamans practise their trickery on clients. A male Sora shaman was once treating an attractive widow. The spirit of the woman's husband spoke through him and told her that the one thing he really missed was spending the night with her and could he do it just once more? She agreed, but of course the only way the husband could make love with her was through the shaman's own body. The shaman slept with the woman, who emerged blameless. The shaman

Three Greenland tupilaks – effigies made to harm a shaman's enemies (right, above, top).

THE SOUND OF A SHAMAN DEPARTING AND RETURNING

"The fire was put out, and there was darkness and total silence. Sitting in a corner of the birch-bark tent, the shaman played quietly on the *domra* (a kind of balalaika) and sang for a long time summoning his spirits. The sound of the *domra* coming from the corner of the tent suddenly started to move about. It sounded first as though it was coming from the centre of the tent, originating at floor level, then it rang out right under the roof and finally seemed to move into the distance, sometimes falling completely silent and then becoming audible once again, approaching slowly from far away. The Khant explained to me in a whisper that the shaman was flying about, calling his spirits.

"And then suddenly in the darkness someone seemed to fly past (as they later explained, this was the shaman flying out of the tent). The tent began to fill with an intriguing rustling noise and suddenly various sounds could be heard, resembling the cries of the birds and animals. First we heard the sound of the cuckoo: 'cuckoo, cuckoo!' Its soft, melodious song could be heard for some time in different corners of the tent. Then the sad and delicate song of the cuckoo was suddenly replaced by the flapping of the wings of an enormous owl: 'kho, kho, kho, kho!' This ill-omened hooting literally filled the tent and made a forceful impact on the mood of the audience, especially in the complete darkness. After this there was the cry of the hoopoe: 'khudo, khu-do!' At this my neighbours anxiously whispered, 'A hoopoe, a hoopoe, oh dear!'

"Suddenly this grim picture was broken by the rousing and cheerful cry of startled ducks: 'krya, krya, krya!' The mood of the audience immediately changed, and they whispered happily and heaved sighs of relief. Then the chatter of a squirrel rang out. It seemed to be leaping from one tree to another. The people sitting in the tent were surrounded by a whole crowd of spirits in the form of birds and animals. Now was the moment for divination. When the squirrel appeared someone said, 'Squirrel, I am going to shoot you – fall down!' The sound of a squirrel falling out of a tree foretold a good hunt. But if the squirrel began to chatter more loudly and to jump about more, that meant an unsuccessful hunt.

"And then suddenly someone seemed to fly into the tent from above, and again the sound of the *domra* and the song of the shaman could be heard. This meant that he had returned from his mysterious, distant wanderings. And again it seemed as if the *domra* was playing in different parts of the tent one after another, under the roof or else at some distance. Unexpectedly under the gentle accompaniment of the *domra*, there arose the beautiful song of a girl who seemed to be approaching slowly from afar... "

A Russian traveller called Shatilov, describing a Khant seance, quoted in Basilov, 1984.

was admired for his imaginative trick.

A person who can persuade spirits to cure someone can also persuade them to attack, and in many traditions the role of healer and sorcerer are merged. An Alaskan Eskimo shaman once "drowned" an effigy of his rival and during the next whaling season this rival was dragged under water by a harpoon line. Such shamans used to collect the bones, skins and sinews of dead animals, breathe life into them and send them on deadly missions. This sorcery was called *tupitkaq*, a word which is also used to refer to the positive process

A Nepalese shaman cures with fire, by setting a brush alight and using it to beat the patient

of bringing the whalebone-framed igloo alive during the whaling season, an action which is essential for generating the whales to be hunted.

The uncertainties which shamans can feel about their own tricks is revealed by the story of Quesalid, a Kwakiutl man from Vancouver in Canada. Quesalid was convinced that shamans were merely conjurers and frauds, and set out to unmask them by the unusual path of apprenticing himself to them in order to learn their tricks. And indeed, they did teach him how to pretend to faint, to make himself vomit, and to use spies to pick up medical and personal details about patients. They also taught him their greatest trick, to hide a tuft of down in his mouth, suck the patient's body, then bite his tongue so that the down became soaked in blood. The shaman then vomited the bloody down and presented it to the patient as a worm representing the illness which he has extracted. However, events forced Quesalid to practise as a shaman and he was unnerved to find himself resoundingly successful. He became famous, yet continued to believe himself to be a fraud who succeeded only because the patient believed in him. In his contests with other shamans, Quesalid triumphed time after time and healed their incurable patients. His rivals confessed their trickery, were humiliated, went mad and died, but Quesalid continued his now inescapable career as a great shaman. But his own attitude had changed. He saw the shamans who lacked the bloody worm technique as even more fraudulent than himself, since he at least gave the patient a tangible representation of the illness while they give the patient nothing. Perhaps there were spirits helping him. So even while practising his own false craft, Quesalid was no longer so certain that real shamans did not exist.

The shamanic trickster survives in popular culture as the harlequin.

Shamans may give an outer demonstration of their inner experiences in many ways. Here a Huichol shaman from Mexico demonstrates his state of spiritual equilibrium by "flying" about from rock to rock at the edge of a waterfall.

The shaman's multiple nature

Shamans are central figures in their societies, yet they are also marginal, marked off from others by the extraordinary nature of their experiences and personalities. Even if shamans are ordinary hunters, housewives or farmers when off-duty, they retain the constant potential to enter other worlds and become other beings. Their different identities are often opposed in pairs and expressed simultaneously during rituals: the shaman is both healer and sorcerer, human and divine, human and animal, male and female. The sum of each paired term indicates the totality of the shaman's way of being.

The shaman has a double nature as both human and divine because he or she incarnates the spirits in his or her own body. This is quite unlike a priest, for whom impersonating Allah, Jehovah or the Holy Ghost is inconceivable or even blasphemous. The shaman becomes spirit, like a possessed person, but is always in control of the incarnation.

Similarly, the shaman can become a fish or a bird, a reindeer or a whale. In Amazonia, a shaman can become a jaguar by taking an exceptionally large dose of *viho* snuff. When he dies, the shaman may turn permanently into a jaguar. An identical belief about tigers is found among the Batek and Temiar of Malaysia.

Shamans may also be able to mediate in complex ways between classes and

An antler hat which was worn by a Siberian shaman in order to emulate the powers of the deer.

ethnic groups. The lowly tribal Sora shamans gain their powers by marrying high-caste Hindu spirits, opening up a perspective which allows the Sora to unravel and explore the tensions in their troubled relations with neighbouring peoples. Shamanism in Latin America, in particular, seems preoccupied with the trauma of colonial power and with the violence of relations between Indians and whites.

A shaman also has a complex personality by virtue of the drama of his or her performance. The shaman does not suffer from a multiple personality in the sense of a psychotic illness, because this sense of multiple personality implies a world of private fantasy whereas the shaman's spirits concern the community at large. As well as the shaman's own spirits it is the gods, nature spirits, waterfalls, ancient ancestors and recently deceased loved ones of the community whom the shaman incarnates, playing on the audience's own feelings of tenderness and fear. The widespread use of masks, disguises and animal costumes underlines the extent to which the persona presented is not the shaman's own.

A Sora shaman and her apprentice may sing a song in unison which alludes to "tightrope paths" and also to "your monkey's four-footed walks, grandmother". The "grandmothers" referred to in the song are helper spirits who were once living

Sora shamans. These previous shamans become monkeys and help the present shamans on the difficult path to the underworld. In order to clamber to the underworld, the living shamans slip out of their bodies and their souls also turn to monkeys.

Shamanic societies recognize many strands which go to make up a person and which do not correspond simply to the European components of body and mind, or soul. For example, each of the different parts of the body in Mongolia has its own *ezhin*, a spirit "Master" or "Owner". In modern psychological terms, the shaman's helpers resemble the alter ego or other similar "projections". That is, they can be interpreted as aspects of the total self, arising through one's personal history and relationships with others and experienced as being external.

Thus shamans often send familiar spirits to do a job, whether of healing or of sorcery, rather than going themselves. Again, the Sora shaman's own soul is absent in the underworld during trance but her place is taken by the

A vegetalista *shaman with a macaw hat, boa-skin jacket, ray-fish trousers and armadillo feet, representing his ability to move freely between the realms of air, earth and water. He stands on a ball of gas, ready to levitate up a glass tube. Layer upon layer of subaquatic worlds can be seen through the hole below.*

voice of her own teacher and predecessor, with the extra authority which this brings. The Washo shaman Henry used to visit a high school which owned a skeleton of a Hindu. One day its spirit entered (or "got on") Henry and thereafter became one of his main helpers. After this, Henry gradually came to form a new picture of himself when healing. While sitting alongside the patient, he envisioned himself moving around the patient's body in the form of a skeleton with a turban on its head.

The Wana canoe journey can take two different forms which reveal clearly how interchangeable the shaman's identity can be with that of his spirit helpers. In one form, the shaman recounts the journey in song but it is his helper spirits who propel the boat, negotiate with the Owner in the sky and rescue the patients' souls. In the other form, instead of being slowly propelled by a crew of spirit oarsmen, he leads his helpers himself along the path of the

According to the Canadian Inuit, when all is right with the world, animal inue *(people) reach out to each other in harmony. The* inue *below were drawn by a shaman from Baker Lake.*

wind, of the blinking of an eye, or of a flash of lightning.

Whether we see spirit helpers as external or internal to the shaman must depend on our initial assumptions about reality. But either way, we can recognize that this is a way of talking about the size or scope of the person. Whatever minimum core the person is thought to have, these spirits represent an augmentation of that person. A psychological approach, which sees spirits as a metaphor for something inside the mind, stretches our idea of the person to encompass them, while shamans and their societies conceive them as lying outside the person and entering into relations of association and alliance.

The Siberian shaman summons spirits from all quarters with the sound of his drum, which he then uses to gather them up. The spirits are scattered aspects of the shaman's self – or rather, since this might imply pathology, they are scattered extra aspects of whatever it is that gives the shaman a much larger personhood than ordinary people, containing as he does all his own past, everybody else's past, their inner feelings and the sentience of the surroundings. The phrase "mastery of spirits" is not always appropriate since the relationship between shaman and spirit can be an uncertain one, and the shaman's anguish can be too intense to justify the name of master.

TRANSVESTITE SHAMANS

Transvestism is closely associated with shamanism in many parts of the world. The male Siberian shaman's costume generally contains female symbols, and among the Chukchi of northeastern Siberia, some male shamans became like their female spirits and dressed as women, did women's work and used the special language which was spoken only by women. This can be seen as a marriage with a spirit, but involving a more total identification. At times a male shaman acts out a female role without any cross-dressing. Just across the Bering Strait in Alaska, the Eskimo shaman Asatchaq would take out his *kikituk* effigy by "giving birth" to it. While someone drummed, he would rub his belly until it swelled, pull down his trousers, kneel in the birth position and pull blood from

The berdache *We-Wha stands between the men and the women.*

between his legs, followed by the *kikituk*. Among North American Indians there is a strong tradition of male transvestism, called *berdache*. Among the Navajo the *berdache* is called *nadle*, meaning "one who is transformed", or "changing one". When *berdaches* became shamans they were regarded as exceptionally powerful. The Mohave believed that female shamans were more powerful than male, but that *berdache* shamans were stronger than either. Among the Navajo the *berdaches* had special chants for curing insanity and aiding childbirth and the Lakota and Cheyenne had similar ideas. A knowledge and awareness of the *berdache* tradition has had a significant influence on the gay liberation movement in the USA.

Death of the shaman

In many parts of the world the shaman undergoes a symbolic death during initiation, which is followed by a resurrection. Yakut shamans could be killed and come to life three times. One shaman called No-Jaw was cut into pieces by an enemy and his body scattered, but his spirits gathered him up and brought him back to life. This happened a second time. The third time, No-Jaw tried to run away, but his legs became entangled in a tree-root. His enemy not only cut him up but also threw his jawbone into the fire. The shaman came back to life, received his name of No-Jaw and was given a calf's jawbone as a substitute.

Eventually, the shaman will die in the ordinary sense. Yet the shaman is not simply an individual. He or she is also the bearer of powers which must remain in the world of the living. The shaman received these powers from a predecessor and will hand them on to a successor. This can be done only when a young recruit is ready to receive them. If a Sora shaman cannot find a successor before dying, she may seek out a little girl years after dying and teach her in dreams. The task of finding a suitable

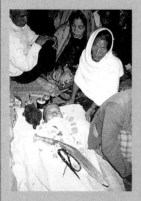

At the funeral of a great Gurung shaman in Nepal, the body is honoured on its way to the grave. At his own request, the shaman is buried cross-legged and with his hands in a position of prayer. He faces north, toward his people's origins in the distant past across the Himalayas. A special rite is performed for the shaman's ancestors and clan gods, and his son and successor adds a special blanket to the grave.

A northwest American Tlingit shaman's four cedar burial boxes, containing his bones and the tools of his trade.

successor can be difficult, and the spirits of a dead shaman can wreak havoc as they rampage through the community seeking a new recruit. In one village in Siberia, the last shaman died in 1992. In the last few years of his life, Communist persecution ceased, but he could not persuade any of his descendants to take on his vocation. With his death, a whole tradition died.

As well as passing on power, a shaman may become a protector spirit and the owner of a site on the landscape. Among the Darkhat Mongols, a shaman would be taken out of the *yurt* (a round tent) and laid in his favourite place. He was left on a stretcher on the ground and his equipment was hung on a nearby tree. It was forbidden to visit the site for 49 days. After three years he was converted from a dangerous spirit into a helpful one. Another shaman would set up a table of offerings and act out the behaviour of the dead shaman as if he had already become a protective spirit, in order to encourage the dead shaman to follow suit. When he was sure that this had happened, the living

shaman passed the spirit into a doll called an *ongon* and hung it in a shrine as a permanent protector.

Where the shaman is feared, the funeral rites may reflect this fear and the spirit's location become an unsafe place. At the burial of a dangerous "black shaman", the Darkhat would break the skin of his drum. Since the shaman was thought to ride his drum through the air like a horse, this immobilized him. When the Yakut shaman No-Jaw was about to die, he told his son to pull him on a sledge to a site by the river. As the son approached the spot, his father suddenly vanished and was never seen again. But now people do not dare to summon their cattle there, for fear that the shaman himself, with his calf's jawbone, will answer.

The burial cairn of a Nepalese shaman, beneath which sits the corpse, holding on to his Life Tree (see p.62). The shaman's gear is hung on the tree. The drum has been slashed and silenced.

Shamans and Clients

The shaman's experience is never just a personal voyage of discovery, but also a service to the community. Through the ordeal of initiation, the shaman is enabled to empathize with the sufferings and needs of others. Being a shaman is probably, in fact, the oldest profession, covering the roles which in industrial societies are played separately by the doctor, psychotherapist, soldier, fortune-teller, priest and politician.

Among the Sora of India, the spirits of a dead boy may enter a shaman and speak to his mother and his other relatives through the shaman's mouth. Not only the resolution of the mother's mourning process but even the inheritance of the boy's belongings will depend on the outcome of the conversations that pass between them. Here the shaman serves not only as a therapist but also as a lawyer, both roles being accomplished through a kind of psychodrama.

In this picture of a group of Sora, the old lady in the centre is a shaman. The spirit of a dead boy has entered her and is speaking to his mother, to the left of the shaman. The mother shows the spirit his silver necklaces and red-fringed loin-cloth which she has lovingly preserved.

Healing the sick, rescuing lost souls

A soul catcher used by a Tlingit shaman to bring back the wandering soul of his patient.

In the shamanic view of the world, illness has only a limited number of possible causes. One or more of a person's souls may be lost, in which case the shaman's soul travels to the realm of the spirits to fight for it and bring it back. Alternatively, there may be a foreign object such as a hairy caterpillar or a splinter of bone lodged in the sufferer's body. This could have been put there by spirits, or else a magic dart could have been fired into the patient by a sorcerer. In this case there is something surplus inside the patient which must be removed. The shaman will suck out the object and perhaps display it to the patient and onlookers. Although trance may be used in such circumstances, a

The face of a Nepalese shaman contorted in effort and concentration as he drums to save the soul of a dangerously sick child. As he drums he chants: "My client has hungered, my client has thirsted. Will you let my client die? Then bring her soul back."

Rubens was only one of many artists to be inspired by the myth of Orpheus, and to paint his own version of the tale (left). This essentially shamanic theme can be found in painters from Titian to Picasso, and in the work of writers and poets from Ezra Pound to Edgar Allen Poe.

ORPHEUS AND EURYDICE

The Greek musician Orpheus, whose harp playing was so exquisite that it made trees uproot themselves to follow him, descended to the underworld in order to rescue his sweetheart, Eurydice, after she trod on a viper and died. He used his music to charm Charon the ferryman, the fierce three-headed guard-dog Cerberus, and the three Judges of the Dead. For a moment, he even soothed the tortures of the damned. He charmed Hades, the king of the underworld, into releasing Eurydice, but only on condition that Orpheus must not look back at her once throughout the entire journey up to the surface. Eurydice followed him through the darkness, guided by his music.

At the last moment, as they were about to emerge into the sunshine, he was so overwhelmed with his love that could not restrain himself from looking back at her, and in doing so, lost her forever.

soul flight is unlikely because the problem is not in the realm of the spirits, but right here in the physical world. If a living enemy is implicated in the cause of an illness, the shaman may try to harm him or her through sorcery, as one way of making the patient stronger is to weaken his or her opponent. Possession and exorcism, in which a spirit inhabits a victim's body and needs to be cast out, do not usually form part of shamanic healing.

Illness can also be caused by the breaking of taboos which are considered basic to morality and good living. Such acts weaken the patient through a withdrawal of vital forces. This kind of misfortune often afflicts whole communities or landscapes, leading to disasters such as crop failure or lack of game. The cure usually involves confession of one's misdeeds.

The shamanic perception of well-being does not only encompass physical health in the medical sense, nor is it restricted to mental health in the psychiatric sense. It includes good nutrition, good friendship, prosperity, and successful business and warfare. All of these things depend on ideas of balance, flow and equilibrium in the environment, and on ideas of giving and withholding, love and anger, and motivation and intention among the spirits which animate this environment.

Whenever a soul is lost, it behaves in ways which often make it sound like an animal. It may have wandered off of its own accord, or have been lured away, or captured and imprisoned. If it has been kidnapped by spirits it may have been taken to another realm. Sometimes the soul is a helpless victim of a violent abduction, in which case the capturing spirit must be fought or outwitted. But often there is some degree of con- nivance, and it is the captured soul itself which must be deceived into allowing itself to be rescued. A Wana woman recounted how on one occasion when she was ill a shaman's spirit helpers on a canoe trip spotted her soul. The soul was attracted by the sound of their drumbeat but then gave them the slip because of its "wild" nature. The patient was a renowned dancer and the spirit helpers encouraged her soul to

An Amazonian Yagua shaman examines his patient prior to entering trance.

dance to show off its skill. Gradually the soul was won over by their flattery and finally it became "tame" and allowed itself to be caught and returned to its owner.

Sometimes the soul is reluctant to be rescued because of an erotic attraction. The *vegetalistas* say that Water People dwell at the bottom of the Amazon in a world of beauty where they use alliga- tors for canoes, turtles for benches and dolphins for policemen. Mermaids dwell there ready to seduce fishermen. When a fisherman succumbs to their

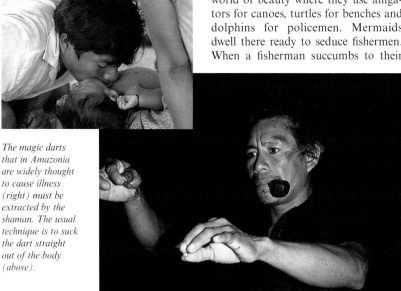

The magic darts that in Amazonia are widely thought to cause illness (right) must be extracted by the shaman. The usual technique is to suck the dart straight out of the body (above).

ESCAPE FROM THE RAVEN-HEADED PEOPLE IN THE SKY

The idea of an opening in the sky was widespread in Siberia and the shaman had to use this route when climbing up into the spirit realm. The Chukchi and Evén thought the hole was located by the Pole Star. Looking down through the hole, one could see the camps of the earth people and watch their women doing the housework. According to the Yakut, a separate sun and moon shone in the upper world and the houses and barns were made of iron. The sky-people had raven heads and human bodies. Once an elderly sky-dweller said to his son, "Go down to the middle world and bring yourself back a wife!" His raven-headed son set off and returned dragging a woman by the hair. They were all happy and held a banquet with dancing while they shut the woman up in an iron barn. Then they heard the sound of a shaman's drum, followed by his singing. The sounds grew louder and then a head appeared from below in the sky-opening. This was the shaman, determined to rescue the soul of the woman who had fallen ill on earth. He put his drumstick to his brow and immediately turned into a bull with a single horn growing from the middle of his forehead. With one blow he smashed the doors of the barn where the woman was imprisoned and disappeared with her down below. A shaman was not always successful, however. On one occasion the spirits of the upper world lit a fire by the opening and stood in readiness. When the shaman appeared in the opening they started beating him with burning logs and drove him back down to earth. (For a psychoanalyst's interpretation of this story, see p.141.)

SHAMANS AND OTHER HEALERS IN SIBERIA

Among the Evén of Siberia, the shaman was sent for only after all ordinary forms and methods of folk medicine had been tried. The functions of a physician were performed by various healers and members of the family. A range of medicines of vegetable and animal origin were a common part of any attempted treatment. The antlers of young reindeer were used as a general tonic, and the blood which spouts out from inside a young antler when it is first cut was considered especially valuable. Other popular medicines were a kind of fern called *oir*, ginseng, and poplar buds which were employed as a painkiller. For liver and stomach diseases, jaundice, dysentery, rheumatism, painful joints, abscesses and ulcers, the healers used bear's gall and

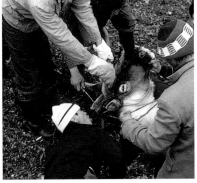

Tungus reindeer herders regaling themselves with fresh blood from the antler of a young reindeer.

musk, a secretion from the stomach glands of the musk-deer. The services of the shaman were only turned to as a last resort.

Shamans are not the only healers in a community. They work alongside herbalists, midwives and bone-setters. There can also be hierarchies of power among shamans themselves. Among the Yakut of northeastern Siberia, the "white" shamans dealt only with the clean, auspicious gods of the sky, while the "black" shamans dealt with the demonic spirits of the lower world. The white shaman prayed instead of going into a trance, and did not kill animals as sacrifices, but consecrated and released them at the *issyakh* festival which marked the traditional New Year, on midsummer's day. The *issyakh* declined under the influences of Christianity and Communism, but has recently been revived.

The rescue of souls may continue after death. A Sora shaman uses a gourd to pour water on the glowing ashes of a funeral pyre. Once the dead person's soul has been cooled in this way it will become capable of speaking to the mourners through the shaman's mouth.

the shaman puts a crucifix to the man's chest and he gradually regains his senses and recognizes his family. The patient is treated with a range of plants and *icaros* that will tie his soul to the land, and although he does not remember anything that happened to him down below, he will never again be allowed to go fishing.

The *vegetalistas* also treat illnesses caused by the intrusion of magic darts called *virote*, which are contained in *yachay*, a special kind of phlegm which shamans and sorcerers can cough up into their mouths and which contains the essence of their power (see p.24). *Virote* are darts, arrows or splinters of bone which are suspended in the

seduction he must be rescued quickly, otherwise he will start to turn into a Water Person and it will become impossible to bring him back. The shaman swallows a preparation of the hallucinogenic vine *ayahuasca* and other plants and sings the *icaro* or chant (see pp.78–79) of a *ninacuru*, an insect with eyes like the headlights of a car. To carry out a reconnaissance the shaman becomes like a *ninacuru*, enters the water and locates the victim in the embrace of a mermaid. The shaman returns to land and finds a colleague for the next journey. They both take *ayahuasca* and enter the water together. While the colleague distracts the mermaid by singing a special mermaid-*icaro*, the first shaman carries the fisherman to land. The rescued man cries and wants to return to the water, but

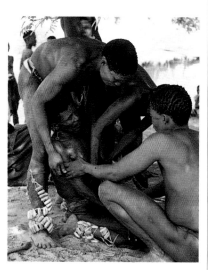

Most San Bushmen can enter a healing trance called kia, *but only a few reach such a deep trance that they can travel up to the sky.*

THE WOMAN WHO WAS SEDUCED BY A MONKEY INCUBUS

Among the Iban of Borneo, many illnesses are attributed to an incubus who abducts or seduces the patient's soul. Incubi are really animals which assume human form and charm their victims, preferably married women, with passionate love songs. A sick woman called Rabai dreamed that she was having sexual intercourse with her husband, but as she awoke in the pale light of dawn she heard the door being opened and noticed her husband still asleep beside her. She had been visited by an incubus who had assumed her husband's form. Her outraged spouse sent word for a very special shaman who had the power to summon evil spirits to appear in the flesh and to engage them in a fight to the death. After a great deal of preparation, the shaman set his trap in an inner room of the house. He unshuttered an opening in the rear wall and laid out a bait of eggs and rice. Then, screened by a curtain of ikat fabric, he waited clutching his spear and sang in the persona of the woman a song of longing to her demon lover:

Calling and crying like a plaintive bird
With the insistent, enticing voice of a lover
These gentle slopes that were bathed at noon
Now call to you
To offer you rice that is sweet and but newly
cooked.

Your darlingest one, day long
She entreats you to come, O Pati Merigi,
To offer you sweet tasting-morsels
As she whispers her yearnings at your waiting
ears.

Then a faint creaking was heard through the curtain, indicating that the incubus had arrived, and the shaman's song changed, as if the creature were squatting in front of its beloved and eating. The shaman leaned out through the curtain, with extreme caution so as not to startle the feeding incubus, for the audience to see him. His smooth, calming song continued but his movements were the movements of a skilled hunter moving in for the kill. He drew back behind the curtain and the tension mounted for another hundred seconds. Suddenly there was the noise of a scuffle and the agonized yelping of a monkey. The audience rushed in and found the room in turmoil. The food was upturned and scattered and a trail of splattered blood led across the floor to the shutter, which was half-torn off its hinge. The monkey, it seemed, had also urinated in its panic. It was mortally wounded and had crawled off into the jungle to die. In the centre of the room, panting, stood the shaman still clutching his spear which was smeared with blood and hairs.

Further incubi that had been molesting other women in the longhouse were killed on the following four nights. An anthropologist who was present obtained samples of the blood and hairs from one of these skirmishes and sent them off for analysis. He received the following reply: "On 24th January, 1951, some hair and smears on glass slides were received for examination from Dr Wallace, Medical Officer in Charge, Third Division. Examinations carried out showed that the hair was monkey's hair and the smears monkey's blood. The specimens are being returned to you please."

---

phlegm and can be fired through the mouth into a distant victim.

In one account a Catholic preacher pierced by a *virote* spends eight months seeking a cure before coming to a *vegetalista* called Don Emilio, who succeeds in healing him. After discussing the circumstances and taking the patient's pulse, Don Emilio rubs camphor and blows tobacco smoke on the affected area and feels around for the dart. He prepares a mixture of three plants which "know each other very well" and then starts to regurgitate the magic phlegm from his stomach. When the phlegm is in his mouth, he spends about an hour sucking the place where the dart has struck, and as he extracts bits of it he spits them in the direction they came from. The plant mixture is used to loosen any remaining effects of witchcraft. The patient will need to return for several more sessions before he is completely cured.

Divining

A Nepalese divination proceeds by questioning a drum.

an integral part of the rescue or soul journey. In parts of northern South America, the shaman sets out to seek advice from his helper spirits on how to cure the patient. The Paviotso shaman in the Great Basin would go on a journey in order to seek a diagnosis and interpret the cause according to the images he saw. If he saw the patient walking among fresh flowers, the prognosis was good, if among faded flowers, then death was inevitable. If he saw that the illness was caused by an intrusive object, he would immediately start sucking it out.

Divination is a means of discovering information which cannot be obtained by ordinary means or in an ordinary state of mind. Although shamans are generally diviners, divining does not necessarily require shamanic powers. Many societies have diviners without having shamans. These may be simply skilled laypersons, like people in the West who read crystal balls and teacups. Among the Even of Siberia, everyone watches the behaviour of animals before setting out on a journey and if they think they see a negative omen, they will abandon the journey for that day. Similarly, they often interpret their dreams as prophetic and listen to the crackling in the fire to find out what will happen the next day. Some people are better at this than others, but they are not necessarily shamans. It seems probable that as the Soviet state eliminated their shamans, divination may actually have increased to fill the vacuum.

The process of divination can also be

Bones are used for divination by people as diverse as the nomads of Mongolia (below) and the Batak of Sumatra (inset).

Divination frequently comes from dreams, either of the patient or of the shaman. The dream may focus on details or give a broad impression. When a Yakut shaman dreamed of having sexual intercourse with a spirit lover, he awoke knowing that he would have a case that day and be successful; if he dreamed of a spirit full of blood and swallowing a patient's soul, he would know that the patient was doomed and would avoid any commissions that day.

A shaman prepares a divination in a courtyard in Taiwan.

Sickness is only one of the many problems that beset humans in an insecure and unpredictable environment. The food supply (see pp.106–8), the fertility of people, animals and crops, bad weather, social relations and difficulties in love all provoke anxiety.

Divination is not only used to address the future, but may also find out what is going on elsewhere in the present. While it seems certain that diviners must be acutely sensitive to clues in the environment and people's behaviour, shamans also use techniques such as asking spirits for information. The Nganasan shaman Dyukhade was asked to locate a man who had been lost in a blizzard for two weeks. "The stalks of withered grass and the bushes around my tent had no knowledge," he explained afterward. "Finally I asked the spirit owner of a stream and on the third day he showed me and I found the man, completely covered in ice but alive."

ASATCHAQ FLIES FROM ALASKA TO SIBERIA

A shaman may be able to see a distant place through clairvoyance, send a messenger there or fly there in person. A young Alaskan Eskimo man had been away a long time trading in Siberia. His father was worried and asked the village shamans to help. The first shaman sent a coloured bead flying off to the island where the young man had last been reported. The bead returned and told the shaman that it had seen red spots like blood by the tents on the island and that the young man must therefore be dead. The second shaman visualized the island through clairvoyance and also saw that it was red. A powerful visiting

shaman from another village, Asatchaq, decided instead to fly there himself.

That night, Asatchaq had his hands tied behind him, wings grew out of his armpits and when the lamp was put out he started to rise out through the ventilation hole and set off towards Siberia. As he flew past a group of tents on the Siberian shore he saw another shaman, his hands bound like his own, flying towards him. Asatchaq tried to ask him for information about the missing youth but his words turned into flames and the other shaman turned round and fled. For a while the two shamans circled the village but Asatchaq feared an attack and moved on quickly until he reached the next camp where the

youth had disappeared. Looking through the hole in a tent top, he saw the young man lying there and put his face to the hole so that the man should recognize him afterwards. So powerful was his flight that when he returned to the worried father's tent he was unable at first to descend to the floor and circled around inside the tent. Finally he collapsed unconscious and when he came to, he said, "Your shamans are fooling you. I have just seen your son lying in a tent and I showed my face to him through the hole." Sure enough, the son returned the next day and said to Asatchaq, "Last night I could not sleep and as I looked up I had a vision; it was your face, in the hole."

Obtaining animals

In hunting societies, catching game is so basic that it has even been argued that it may be an older and more fundamental function than healing. Observing the movements of animals can include the same sort of location techniques as those used by the Alaskan shaman Asatchaq when he had to find a young man who had gone missing (see p.105). These practices seem to be particularly common in northern and Arctic landscapes, where animals constitute practically the only food. In the tropics, some shamanist peoples like the Batek Negrito of Malaysia, for whom hunting is also important, use virtually no hunting magic but simply rely on their knowledge of animal habits. Others, like the peoples of the Amazon, have elaborate ideas about shamans and animal spirits.

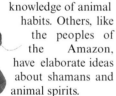

A shaman may be able to locate or lure game because he or she has actually been a game animal.

An Inuit decoy helmet in the shape of a seal.

While one Eskimo man was walking along the shore in Alaska his soul was abducted by a boatload of spirits and taken to the land of the whales. All winter, for eight months, his body lay unconscious in his house. In the spring his soul returned in the form of a whale and allowed itself to be harpooned by his own relatives. He had returned home, and so his body regained consciousness. This experience was his initiation as a shaman, and he became especially adept not only at calling whales but also at dissuading them from giving themselves to enemy

villages, whom he could thereby starve.

For most hunting peoples, the fertility of humans and animals, society and species, are considered to be intimately connected. These links can work by analogy, implying that fertility is in principle unlimited; or through some form of recycling of souls, implying that the store of life-force is somehow finite. The first approach can be seen in parts of Siberia, where the reproduction of game animals was encouraged through dances and mimes representing their rutting and mating. At the instigation of the shaman, a ritual called the "renewal of life" was performed. This involved games such as dancing and wrestling. All the dances, performed by both sexes or by men alone, had an explicitly sexual meaning as they sought to imitate the rutting behaviour

Stones from the American Plains, for calling buffalo.

A Canadian inukshuk – stones piled in human shape to control the movements of caribou.

games themselves.

If, as in the second approach, the life-force is in principle finite, it may be that souls are reborn within the same species, as when Eskimos throw the seal's bladder or kidneys back into the sea. On the other hand, among the Desana of Amazonia, game animals must be bought at the price of human lives. The shaman inhales an hallucinogenic snuff made from the *viho* plant and visits the remote hill-caves of Vai-Mahse, Owner of the Animals. There the animals hang suspended in bunches from the rafters of Vai-Mahse's house, which is thought of as a large animal womb. The shaman negotiates for the release of an agreed number of animals for the season's hunting, according to the orders which the men of his village have placed with him. But in return he promises the souls of a certain number of living people, who must therefore die.

As he walks through the house the shaman shakes the rafters to wake up the animals, who then go out into the jungle. The price of the animal spirits is calculated "per shake", and if the shaman inadvertently wakes up more animals than he has paid for he has to reopen negotiations and promise more human deaths. The people who are to die in this way will not turn into hummingbirds, as with ordinary deaths, but

of male elks and reindeer. The shaman would beat a drum throughout the performance, which was considered not simply fun but also a duty, and use his drumstick to slap the legs of anyone caught slacking. The emphasis was on the virility of both the human community and the animals on which it depended. By their actions the shaman and the hunters had to gladden the spirits animating these species and induce them to play the same kinds of

A caribou or reindeer.

Women in Greenland returning the kidneys of a hunted seal into the sea. This is a major ritual, but is performed quietly. As they slip the kidneys into the water, the women mutter thanks and wishes for more seals under their breaths. In different regions, different parts of the seal are returned to the waters: for example, the bladder in Alaska.

will be returned to replenish Vai-Mahse's store in exchange for the animals which he has allowed the hunters to kill. Although this exchange of souls is essential for the community's survival, it causes some anxiety because people fear the shaman may trade in the souls of those he dislikes. In fact, he generally offers only the souls of other tribes. Disease epidemics that sweep across neighbouring peoples are sometimes attributed to a particularly large deal negotiated by such shamans.

The shaman's role in obtaining animals is obvious in any shamanic society where hunting is still important. Some animal-rights supporters have difficulty understanding the central role of hunting in the lives of many indigenous peoples. In some Eskimo communities, where the harsh landscape allows no other way of life, anti-hunting lobbies have caused social devastation and economic destitution. Modern neo-shamanists, however, with an imagery drawn largely from native North America with its emphasis on spirit helpers and power-animals, are often more comfortable with the culture of hunting.

Yagua tribesmen of South America offering manioc beer to tempt the spirits of the animals they are about to hunt.

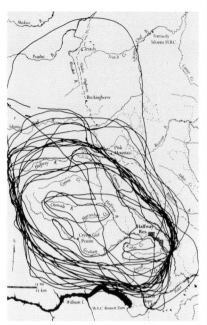

Hunting routes on Halfway River Reserve in Canada, reflecting a mixture of shamanic belief and local knowledge. The routes change to take account of fishing and berry-picking seasons.

ASATCHAQ GOES TO OBTAIN WHALES ON THE MOON

When Asatchaq travelled to the moon, men would anchor him with a stone axe to ensure that his body did not fly away with his soul. When he reached the moon-spirit's igloo, Asatchaq saw tiny caribou running in circles around the houseposts. The people would ask for caribou at new moon and the moon-spirit would let these little caribou fall to earth. On the moon there was also a huge pot of little whales. For a whaler to be successful, his wife had to hold up her own small pot containing water from a pond, said to be the vaginal blood of a mythical woman. The moon-spirit would drop a tiny whale into this pot. The women did indeed have little whale-effigies of lamp-oil tar, said to have been dropped into their pots by the moon. These effigies were believed to gestate inside the pots and were guarded carefully until after the hunt was over.

DYUKHADE MEETS THE MISTRESSES OF THE REINDEER

During the initiation experience of the Siberian shaman, Dyukhade, his stoat and mouse spirit-guides led him to a high mound. He noticed an entrance in the mound and went inside, where he discovered it was light.

There sat two women who looked like reindeer and were covered with fur. On their heads grew branching antlers, and the antlers of one of them were made out of iron. These women were the Mistresses of the Reindeer. They each gave birth to two reindeer calves in front of Dyukhade. The first mistress released her two calves and explained to him that these were to be his sacrificial animals. One of the calves was to serve the needs of the Dolgan and the Evenk people, while the other was for the Nganasan Tavgy. The second reindeer woman released her calves and said that one of these would be wild and that the other would be a domesticated reindeer.

These female divinities explained to Dyukhade that the fertility of all reindeer depended on them. They allowed him to pull one hair from each of them and said, "Put one hair in your right pocket and one in your left. With these you will clothe yourself in a shaman's costume."

An hallucinatory vision drawn by a member of the southern Barasana tribe, one of the Tukano people of Colombia. The vision is induced by drinking a potion made from the yaje *plant, a jungle vine of the* Malpighiaceae *family. The bottom panel shows humankind's first dance. For the first time the Tukano are wearing headdresses made of macaw feathers. They have also painted their bodies and the red and blue dots around them show their generative energy. The top band shows three Masters of Animals separating the animal kingdom into beasts of the water on the right and beasts of the land on the left. Immediately above the animals is the roof over the milky way.*

Protecting the community

The shaman is not a private mystic, but exists to serve a community. For the shaman, the community is generally a fairly small-scale society in which ideas of the soul combine with a cyclical view of natural processes, so that an important part of the shaman's role is to regulate and assist the conservation of the community's soul force. The Evenk of Siberia believed in a clan river which ran around the earth, sky and underworld and along which the souls of deceased clan members passed on their way to being reborn in the same clan. In some Eskimo cultures the name soul is distinct from a person's other souls and returns with the name to a new living being who may or may not be related. Among the Sora, the new bearer of a name is not a reincarnation but may inherit some personality traits from the last person to hold the name. Each lineage has a reservoir of names which are either attached to living persons or are held in trust by ancestors in the underworld, who are only waiting for the birth of a suitable baby to whom they can give their name.

The inclusion of some people in a community or group implies the exclusion of others. Spirits which appear helpful to some people may seem to be hostile to others. The link between shamans and violence is most apparent when communities are at war. The societies which make most use of spirit aggression seem to be quite small, and lacking in a highly formalized social structure or a strong chieftainship.

One such society is the Achuar who inhabit the jungle of the Peru-Ecuador frontier on the upper Amazon. Here there are no fixed communities, but

widely separated single households in an almost permanent state of conflict. There is no cause of illness or misfortune except someone else's aggression, usually in the form of magical darts: even someone who drowns in rapids is believed to have been dragged under by an anaconda sent by a hostile shaman. Here the power to heal depends on the

RIGHT *An Indonesian shaman heals a baby. Young children are the most frequent of the shaman's patients and, as with a western village doctor, his work with successive generations binds him ever more firmly to the community, and vice-versa.*

LEFT *A Sora funeral procession escorts the soul of a dead woman safely home from her husband's village to her father's village for a second burial.*

A tupilak, *a figure created by a shaman from Greenland in order to harm his enemies.*

power to kill. A cure can be effected only by a shaman who possesses an identical kind of dart to that used by the aggressor, which burrows into the patient and draws its fellow dart out into the open by mutual recognition. These darts can never be annihilated or put out of circulation. Their impulse continues indefinitely and the only way to get them out of a patient is to project them into someone else.

In the highlands of New Guinea, the Baruya live in a similar situation. Healing and warfare fuel each other in a never-ending cycle, since illness is caused by a magic projectile sent from an enemy village and the patient can be healed only by returning the projectile back to its sender. Shamans work night after night to extract splinters of bone, stone or cassowary feather from their fellow-villagers and fire them back to the village from which they came.

As a person with extraordinary powers, the shaman may need to be held in check by the society he or she serves. Both Baruya and Achuar shamans are considered unreliable. More Achuar shamans are murdered by their neighbours than killed by rivals' darts, while Baruya shamans cannot keep full control over their magic arrows or spirit doubles, which sometimes turn against their own people. In both societies, a shaman could not avoid attacking people because this would also amount to a refusal to heal.

Many traditional societies see sorcery as integrally related to healing. In other societies, the roles of healer and sorcerer are distinguished, at least in principle. The Sora sorcerer is an inversion and perversion of the healing shaman. Yet when the Washo shaman, Henry, received a vision which steered him exclusively towards healing and good actions, it was against a back-

ground of tradition in which shamans were expected to be sorcerers as well.

The shaman's techniques as such are morally neutral, but within the community much shamanic activity is concerned with morality, and many areas of social behaviour may be regulated and arbitrated through the shaman. In this respect the shaman is not so much a psychotherapist as a sociotherapist. When the *vegetalista's* patient was wrenched from his mermaid lover, restored to his family and forbidden ever to go fishing again, the diagnosis and treatment were a reminder of a

AN EVENK SHAMAN'S-EYE VIEW OF ATTACK, CURE AND COUNTER-ATTACK

Running through the centre of the picture is the Podkamennaya Tunguska river (1) with its tributaries (2). The territory of the Momol clan is marked by (3), showing the clan's sacred ceremonial tree (4), the Mistress of the clan's territory (5) and the clan's reindeer guardian spirit (6). The entire territory is protected by a fence of spirit watchmen (7). Across the river to the top of the picture is the territory of the Nyurumnal clan (8) with their own ceremonial tree, Mistress of the territory and reindeer guardian spirit (9, 10, 11). The Nyurumnal clan likewise have their fence of spirit watchmen (12).

The action begins in the Nyurumnal shaman's tent (13) where we see the shaman and his assistants (14, 15) sending an attacking spirit into Momol territory to destroy the Momols. A wavy line (16) shows the path of this spirit, which penetrates unnoticed and unchallenged past the Momol clan's spirit fence (7), changes into a wood-boring worm, enters the entrails of a member of the Momol clan (17) and begins to destroy his corporeal body. The victim is shown inside his tent (18) with his wife (19). Now the action shifts to the Momol shaman's tent (20). The shaman, surrounded by clan members (21, 22), starts to divine to find out the cause of the sickness. The shaman sends a spirit goose and snipe (23, 24) to the patient with orders to extract the

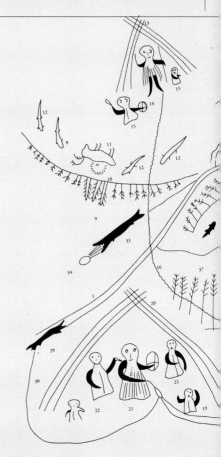

man's duty to stay with his family. Not even shamans are immune from the moral control of their own system. The *vegetalista* and the Baruya shamans who extract a magic dart will return it to its sender, who may be killed by it if hit unexpectedly. The Sora sorcerer's spirits can never have enough victims to feed on and eventually turn on and consume the sorcerer. This is interpreted as moral justice: the spirits are evil, but the result is good. As the Sora say, "The fire has blown back on him".

A very prominent mechanism of morality is taboo and punishment. The

In order to create a harm-bringing tupilak, *a shaman may use human bones taken from graves, and often including a child's skull. He will pack these in hide, and bring them to life. The drawing was made in Greenland, in 1915.*

worm. Their path is shown at (25). They poke their beaks into the sick man's entrails but the disease spirit jumps out of the patient and tries to escape. The shaman sends some more helpers to catch it. A splintered spirit-pole clutches the spirit and holds it, while a spirit knife stands by (26). The shaman then orders a spirit owl (27) to swallow the disease spirit, carry it to the abyss of the lower world and release it through an opening like an anus (28).

Now follows revenge. The Momol shaman sends a two-headed pike (29) to attack the Nyurumnals along the track shown at (30). Inside a Nyurumnal tent (31) the pike spirit attacks its victim (32) and carries off that person's corporeal soul (33, 34). Meanwhile the Momol shaman reinforces his people's defences by building a further fence of larch spirits (35), overseen by guards made of splintered poles (36), across the point where the Nyurumnal shaman's spirit had originally penetrated his defences. Finally, animals are sacrificed to the Momol clan's own spirits and their skins hung up (37, 38).

This picture shows both ordinary and shamanic reality, as well as a succession of events making up a total drama in which the shaman is the key player. It also shows how closely Evenk shamanism was bound up with the community. If war is diplomacy by other means, here we see how shamanism can also function as warfare by other means, and that its healing side appears inseparable from what we must call sorcery.

punishments often appear disproportionately harsh for what might seem a minor offence, but the actions are more than they seem. A Wana woman's menstrual blood must not be burned because it is the source of human life. In some Eskimo settlements, the seal's bladder must not be eaten, or thrown to the dogs, but must be returned to the sea because it is from this that another seal will be regenerated. These actions represent both a sense of aesthetics and a powerful respect for the preciousness of life, in a context where human actions are believed to affect it. It is in the nature of an integrated view of the universe that a wrong action in one realm may have a bad consequence in another. Acts like murder and incest damage the single structure which encompasses living humans, social groups, ancestors, spirits, animals, plants, landscape and elements. Diagnosis and treatment re-establish that single moral universe and this act of repair is seen as a cleansing of "pollution". Thus a sick person is a sign of a fault in the cosmos, so that both tend to be healed together.

ASATCHAQ'S DUEL WITH A SHAMAN FROM SIBERIA

After he flew to Siberia to find his host's missing son (see p.105), Asatchaq became famous in that part of Alaska. He was on a later visit there with his wife when another shaman came across the ice from Siberia on a dog-sledge. The Siberian shaman had heard that there was a great shaman on the Alaskan side and wanted to compete with him. That evening, the Siberian started to perform. He cut off his tongue, swallowed part of it and gave the rest to the dogs. Then he gouged out his own eye, ate all of it except the iris and threw that to the dogs. As a wind blew in through the entrance of the house, it brought the parts of his body back into place. Then the Siberian started to drum and the lamps were put out. He summoned his spirit helper and Asatchaq's wife felt so ill that she started to die. Asatchaq began to revive her while the Siberian boasted that he could kill anyone he wished. Then Asatchaq produced his *kikituk* and walked around the house stopping at every sick person and making the effigy gnash its teeth at them, which was his standard method of healing. When the Siberian shaman was off his guard, Asatchaq jabbed the *kikituk* several times into his back. The next afternoon, he heard that the Siberian was dead, but the local villagers knew that in his own country he had often died and come to life again a few days later. Asatchaq took no chances but left his *kikituk* in the shaman's body for half a month before retrieving it.

A vegetalista *vision-painting from Peru, showing three* vegetalistas *who have gathered to take the drug,* ayahuasca. *The man on the left, dressed in steel scales and with a red aura, is a sorcerer who never heals, only kills. The man dressed in green is a witch and a sorcerer, who casts spells to imprison people and do with them as he pleases. The man dressed in blue is a "perfect master", who only heals. He carries glass arrows and a bow, in case he needs them, but should he ever use his weapons he becomes a criminal.*

In some Sora villages, each descendant of a dead person contributes some rice-flour, which the shaman then makes into an effigy representing the deceased. The shaman infuses some of the dead person's soul into the effigy, which is subsequently cooked and swallowed by the descendants. Through this act of symbolic cannibalism the name of the deceased will now reappear among one of the descendants.

Shamans and the state

Just as shamans do not function except in a society, so they do not work in a political vacuum. Shamanism is not timeless: all forms of shamanism that are known of have changed constantly as they have been affected by contacts between peoples, struggles for territory, inter-tribal warfare, the growth and collapse of empires or the imposed world-views of colonialism.

This fact is indisputable, but is often ignored. The most influential book on shamanism ever written, that by Eliade, presents shamanism as an archetype with an apparently timeless quality or essence. Although he is a historian of religions, Eliade's version of shamanism appears to stand outside political history. Such a standpoint allows him to label different forms of shamanism as more and less authentic (for example, techniques using hallucinogens are considered a mark of degeneracy).

Closer attention to political context, however, shows that Eliade's archetypal forms emerge from diverse and competing political and religious practices which closely reflect the struggles and strategies of the moment. Too close a focus on the shaman's initiation and career may simply repress our awareness of history.

Political power resides in the ability to control other people's actions, so that it is not only spiritual power which is based on ideas of fertility, blessing, ancestry and helper spirits. In the kinds of society where people widely believe in such things, they are also the foundation of political power. Genghis Khan's justification for trying to conquer the world, and massacring the populations which stood in his path, lay in his supposed descent from the god of the sky. Indeed, at the same time as being the most archetypal region for Eliade's classic shamanism, Mongolia, south Siberia and Central Asia have been most deeply involved in the rise and fall of empires. While tribes of Tungus hunters moved nomadically across the forests of eastern and northern Asia, their close relatives, the Manchu, sat on the heavenly throne of the Chinese empire in Peking from 1644 until 1911, and tried to reproduce at court the shamanic system

The Emperor P'u-i was the last of the Manchu dynasty that ruled China for more than 250 years. Although P'u-i himself wished to embrace a modern, western lifestyle (he was also known as Henry), his position as Emperor forced him to adopt the role of a shamanic oracle. He was tried as a war criminal by the Mao government in 1950.

of their wild forest cousins.

What are the various political contexts in which shamans function? It is helpful to consider this in terms of the shaman's relationship to the state. Societies without a state, such as groups of hunters, may have a chief as well as a shaman, or else the shaman may also be a charismatic leader and warrior. The Achuar of Amazonia and the Baruya of New Guinea show a mixture of these types of leader. They have "Big Men", or prominent warriors, but it is the instability of this kind of "chieftainship" which fuels their chronic warfare and gives the shaman's magical powers of aggression such prominence.

Wars take place between villages or clans even within a larger state, such as happened among the Evenk within the Russian empire and the Soviet Union. This is a way of relating to other, similar groups without passing through the machinery of the state itself. One reason why Sora shamanism does not include this kind of warfare sorcery may be that the Sora are in sufficiently close contact with the outside world that they can now attack each other by using lawyers from the nearby town or denouncing each other to the police.

Where people's political relationships are tied up with the state, their access to the divine also takes place through a correspondingly bureaucratic idiom. Throughout Asia, helpers are sometimes spirits of the wild, but are very often also kings, policemen, generals and clerks at government offices where identity documents and permits are sought and obtained. One Sora shaman who lived under the British empire says that his spirits are more powerful than any other shaman's because they are not mere Hindu clerks who write by hand but white typists. Away from state power, the shaman's battle or negotiation takes place with a being who is powerful but in some ways an equal, as in a hunter's relationship with his prey. As the community is drawn further into the state this relationship is replaced by a humble petition at the feet of an emperor in the sky or the underworld. While the forms of shamanism are otherwise similar, the Masters of the spirit realm among the small northern Siberian groups are replaced in south Siberia and Central Asia by a spirit Khan or Emperor.

Few, if any, shamanisms have avoided incorporating an awareness of state power, and where contacts between shamanic communities and the state are close, such communities are often marginalized from the dominant culture or the capital. In these situations shamanism, like possession cults, may be opposed to an established priesthood, as happens so clearly in the Indian culture area (see pp.38–41).

Another response to political domination is for shamanism to act as a mark of distinctive ethnic identity or even as a focus of resistance. In cases such as these shamanism may be not so much weak as anti-centrist – perhaps in

A Sora idtal, *or shamanic drawing, showing officials and spirits carrying rifles.*

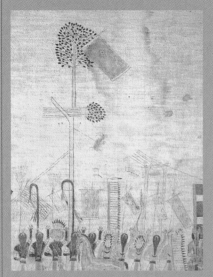

A Plains Indian painting of a Sun Dance.

keeping with its hunting origin – and subversive. The picture of the Hindu world revealed in Sora shamanism often amounts to a satire or a parody. Shamanism was widely persecuted in the Communist world (see pp.136–7).

A more forceful resistance occurred in the Ghost Dance of the Indians of the Great Basin and the plains in 1889–90. This was partly a transformation in religious experience and expression, under the pressure of political circumstances. After the military onslaught of the US Cavalry and the extermination of the bison by white hunters, the Sun Dance could no longer keep its earlier function of seeking supernatural help in warfare and hunting. Many leading Sun Dancers turned to the Ghost Dance religion. The founder of this movement was told by God in a vision that the dead would return, bringing back with them the good old days. To make this happen, the Indians were to dance the local style

of round dance for days on end, an action which led to many people collapsing from exhaustion and experiencing visions themselves. Among the more warlike tribes, the movement took on an anti-white tone and ended in 1890 with the brutal massacre of Chief Sitting Bull and the Sioux dancers at Wounded Knee. Other groups of Sun Dancers learned the lesson of this slaughter. Turning away from any political quest, they redirected their emphasis to healing sickness and promoting the spiritual health of the community.

Similarly, shamanism may become particularly associated with women, as in much of eastern Asia where it has been subordinated to a Buddhist or Confucian High Culture which is more male-centred. Its status need not be seen as inferior. In Lewis's classic argument, the preponderance of women in possession cults worldwide provides a front for a "feminist subculture" in which women protest obliquely at a male-centred world. In her study of Korean female shamans Kendall disputes this, arguing that the family gods and ghosts dealt with by women are an

Divining by means of a sword. The sword is stood up in a bowl of uncooked rice – if it remains standing, the answer to the question is positive.

In Nepal, shamans play an active part in local politics, such as this village meeting.

integral part of Korean religious and social life and that women's religion provides an indispensable specialized complement to that of men.

Shamanism may be part of a battle for control of the state, or at least held in dynamic tension with other kinds of power. The arrival of white colonial power did not always lead to the spectacular, unexpected breakup of native societies, but only highlighted tensions that were already latent within the indigenous systems. Where there were already two different focuses of power, such as shamans and chiefs, the chiefs were sometimes incorporated into the structure of the colonial state while the shamans were forced to the margins and persecuted, or else became the focus for a resistance movement.

Alternatively, shamanic power may become concentrated at the centre and the figure of the shaman itself centralized. In the Manchu empire, most kinds of shaman remained in the forests of northern Manchuria while clan shamans came to court and evolved into little more than priests, unable to enter trance at all. Shamanic guardian spirits such as the white pheasant became mere heraldic devices on army uniforms. An 18th-century emperor decided to revive the tradition of shamanism as central to Manchu identity by writing it all down. The result was to create a shamanic state religion which lasted until 1911, but one in which all the dynamic and expressive elements of the old oral tradition were smothered in the complicated ritual texts and civilized manners of Confucian court etiquette.

CELESTIAL KINGS IN THE SUBURBS OF KOREA

A senior shaman in Korea instructs her apprentice in how to dance: "When the Heavenly King appears, you show his crown like this. When you've got his message, when you see what he wants, you say, 'I'm the Heavenly King, why haven't you done this for me?' Or someone with pockmarks takes shape in your eye, she's Princess Hogu, isn't she? And all the Generals from long ago look like this." She places her hands on her hips and thrusts her chest forward imperiously. Other spirits she might call up include the Knife-Riding General. This courtly symbolism is a long way from the practises of the jungle and forest peoples on the outer fringes of the old kingdoms and empires of Asia.

A Korean shaman dances ecstatically as she manifests the Warrior Spirit. The banknotes beside her head are her payment.

Dramas and roles

The smell of food being prepared, the sweat of the audience packed closely together, the atmosphere of expectation or fear, the joking, the distractions of children cutting across the arena, the music, song, dance, drama and mime – all these are inextricably entwined with the methods of ritual to produce the full experience of the shamanic rite. Consider the scene at a funeral as a Sora shaman sits down to go into trance, against the throbbing of drums and the pounding of feet among people crushed shoulder to shoulder inside the tiny mud house. According to the mood of the occasion and the degree of their personal involvement, some people squat on their haunches and huddle intently around the shaman arguing vehemently with the dead as they appear one at a time and speak to them through her mouth, weeping and embracing her as she is momentarily filled with the spirit of someone they loved. A number of people come and go at the edge of the proceedings and interpose the occasional careless remark, while others crack irreverent jokes to the accompaniment of loud guffaws. From one funeral to the next, and on many ritual occasions in between, various goupings of people find themselves in constantly recurring contact as they continue to develop their complex personal and social relations long after

A bear mask from northwest America.

The mask of a wrinkled old man, used in curing rites.

A mask worn by a Kwakiutl shaman in a cannibal dance.

some of their number have crossed the dividing line between life and death.

The initiation or vision quest, and the maintenance of relations with his or her helper spirits, involve the shaman in long periods of solitude. This led Eliade to see shamanism as a "mysticism ... at the disposal of a particular elite". But being a shaman is ultimately a public role and the shaman's inner experience reaches its culmination and its full significance only as part of public performance. To say that shamanic action is sometimes highly theatrical is not to imply that the shaman is "only acting", as though this were something false. Rather, the performance transforms the inner reality or consciousness of a whole range of people who are involved in a number of different ways. It is this which makes the question of trickery irrelevant. Items of equipment are in one sense theatrical props, but they are also genuine expressions or extensions of the shaman's persona. Is a shaman who wears a mask or speaks with the voice of a god or an ancestor a true incarnator or a mere dramatist? A shaman who impersonates someone else is simultaneously both him- or herself – that is, an ordinary mortal – and a spiritually empowered being. When this shaman engages the audience, they are called upon to respond to a figure who resembles someone they know but whose consciousness has been transformed through a powerful association with spirits. The audience is sometimes even able to test this paradox, as when they put a Sora shaman's baby to her breast while she is incarnating a male ancestor (see p.65).

Shamanic performance is a highly skilled activity in which the delicate collective mood is vulnerable to collapse, resulting in the failure of the purpose of the ritual. In this light, healing power is a form of artistry. The Kwakiutl, Quesalid, became a great shaman because he performed as one and it was his success at performing which gave him the power to cure (see pp.89–90).

There are gradations of theatricality and expertise, just as there are gradations of shaman. In many parts of the world, shamans are not distinguished sharply from other people who have some degree of the same skills, such as diviners. The term "shamanship" is helpful here, since it suggests a talent or inclination like musicianship or craftsmanship which is spread variously among different persons. The shaman gives a full-scale

A performer from the Kaos theatre company.

dramatization to the many little mimes and performances which occur in everyday life.

"Parents have to be half shamans to raise up their children," said a Korean woman as she lunged with a kitchen knife at the invisible, baleful forces in the air above her daughter's pillow and then lured them into a gourd dipper baited with millet, before tipping the entire dipper out at a safe distance from the house. Some Sora laypersons know all the words of shamans' songs but are simply unable to act them out and make them work as performance. Similarly, Kendall has movingly documented the attempts of a young Korean woman, Chini, to act out her initiation as a shaman. Her own state of faith regarding her spirits is not clear but whatever it is, she is unable to make the leap from this to successful performance.

Some leading neo-shamanists have taken anthropologists to task for an overemphasis on shamanic performance, arguing that it leads them to concentrate on the superficial form rather than the spiritual content of much shamanic activity because they are reluctant to treat the shamans' experiences of spirits as real and discuss these instead. While the neo-shamanists are surely right in this, the problem lies in an incompatibility between views of reality rather than in the notion of performance itself.

"Non-rational" theatre takes inspiration from shamanism, Japanese Butoh and the Theatre of Cruelty.

A performance divorced from text or character.

A Nepalese shaman dances around the "world mat" – on which chaff is separated from grain – in an effort to find a patient's departed soul (below). The shaman who spots the soul (above) is staring off into the other world.

The view of performance which they condemn presupposes a separation of the shaman from the audience which is found only in some highly formalized traditions of theatre. However, if daily life is seen as a kind of drama in which every participant has a role, then a shamanic performance becomes simply an intensified form of this.

In a shamanic performance the shaman interacts with the spirits, the immediate patient, and also with the wider audience, which amounts in some sense to society itself. The shaman's relationships with spirits and with patients are respectively the focus of different phenomenological and therapeutic interpretations (see pp.70–73 and 98–103). It is also possible to explore the question of how far familiar spirits may be considered an expression of the shaman's relation with aspects of his or her own self.

The involvement of shaman and audience has recently been explored in performance theory. Here, shamanic ritual appears close to post-modern theatre, in which the performance is not

Korean shamans become the Mountain God to berate a client (left) and perform divination (right).

a finished product but a continuing process of self-expression. Many anthropological approaches imply that ritual performance acts out some hidden cultural script, but it is perhaps more appropriate to suggest that the culture itself is constantly being formed and reformed through these performances. The narrative force of shamans' accounts of their initiations, journeys and battles, the initial uncertainty and step-by-step detection work of divinations and confessions, all make it clear that something vital is being created on the spot by a collective consensus as the performance proceeds.

There are important levels on which the roles of shaman, patient and audience cannot be sharply distinguished. A rite to heal one sick person is also a rite to ensure the continued good health of the group. The mutual involvement of persons in shamanistic societies often ties their perceptions and their fates very closely together. When a group of Sora crowd around a shaman to argue with an attacking spirit and defend their sick relative, they also know that if the patient dies, he or she will become an aggressive spirit which will pass on its own terminal sickness to those who remain alive. Similarly, the shaman's initiation is an inner drama which must somehow also be witnessed by the public. Shamans are constantly judged for their effectiveness. Atkinson's study of the Wana of Indonesia shows how shamans must continually use performance in order to prove their shamanship and to win public confidence.

THE NEED TO PERFORM

In Siberia, some shamans suffer if they have not performed for a long time. Recently among the Evenk a female shaman fell ill and asked another herdswoman to heat a piece of iron until it was red hot and then give it to her. She took it and began to lick it and the iron hissed until it became cold. The shaman said that her soul felt at ease at last, she fell into a deep sleep and awoke the next morning fit and healthy again. Although he is not a shaman, her son sometimes has the same need.

DIAGNOSIS BY DANCE

A Yakut shaman sets out dancing after a woman's sick soul by springing like his reindeer spirit mount and tapping himself with a stick as he goes. He dismounts, ties up his deer and continues on foot. Then he becomes a hawk, flies and lands. Meanwhile his reindeer and the reindeer-vehicle of the evil spirit engage in battle, while the shaman slips off to look at the condition of the patient's soul and dances his reaction to the state of the patient, whether curable or doomed.

THE MANY PEOPLE AFFECTED BY A SHAMAN'S PERFORMANCE: THE WOMAN WHO DIES TO SAVE HER BABY

The following extract from a dialogue between the living and the dead among the Sora gives a glimpse of the wide range of persons whose lives can be involved in a shamanic performance. The words are spoken through the mouth of a frail old female shaman nicknamed Rondang, meaning "Bag of Bones". The dead woman, Panderi, was a young wife who died suddenly after carrying her baby through the jungle. At first Panderi tells how closely integrated she felt in the family of her husband, whom she married only recently and with whom she was very much in love. Her husband is present but too overcome with grief to speak and the dead woman converses with his female relatives:

Panderi (dead woman): [faintly] I got eaten up, I got drunk up, mothers [describing the action of an attacking spirit].
Mother-in-law (living): Ah my dear, it was so sudden, just like that, you ... *[continues inaudibly]*.
Panderi: After I came and joined your group, mothers ...
Mother-in-law: [rising out of inaudibility] Yes, "this is my house, my home" you said ... Have a drink before you go.
Panderi: [same small, shaken voice] O dear, really I got eaten up, I got drunk up.
Mother-in-law: [near-inaudible monotone] Didn't we do all your healing rites and sacrifices whenever you needed them? Yet if only you'd been ill first we could have done something this time. Didn't we do all your sacrifices?
[It emerges that Panderi was killed by a gang of spirits who had intended to kill her baby, who is the only son and heir of her husband's family, but that she bent over to protect him and the spirits killed her instead.]
Panderi: It's not that; but your little grandchild would have been swallowed right up and I would still have been alive. I bent down to protect him, mothers, and they ate me up instead.
Mother-in-law: Yes, if they'd got the child, you'd have been all right.
Panderi: Yes, they ate me right up. *[Calling out:]* "Ah, really, help me, fathers, Ah, really,

help me!", I cried, "Ah aunts, Ah uncles, Ah mothers-in-law, Ah fathers-in-law!"
Mother-in-law: How could we see you?
[Not only does Panderi feel close to her husband's family, she actually defied her own family in order to marry him. Her family disapproved of the match because the couple were cousins of a prohibited degree. The day she died her brothers brushed her husband aside and plundered the couple's house for her personal ornaments on the assumption that the baby would not survive to inherit them since other women will not breastfeed orphans.]
Panderi: [tearful] "Where's my husband, where's my husband, I want to be with him, I want to speak to him, where's your nephew, where's your son?" is all I cried. *[Quiet again:]* They ate me up fresh-and-alive. *[Fast hysterical monotone:]* "Ah husband, Ah spouse, now that we've stopped being cousins, you do my sacrifices instead of my brothers. Ah fathers, Ah mothers!" I said – *[her mother-in-law is speaking very fast in the background, words inaudible]* Your child, your grandchild, they would have beaten him and snatched him, but I screamed, "O gai, my baby! O gai, my baby!" and bent down over him, so they ate me up instead.

At the inquest it emerges step by step that the gang of dead people who ate and drank Panderi was led by one of her husband's cousins who stands in exactly the same relationship to him as do Panderi's family. The attacker is understood as a symbolic representation of her own family and the attack is seen as a fulfilment of their wish to destroy her marriage. This wish was also partly acted out by her brothers when they took back their sister's ornaments. But for the moment the baby is still alive and the husband goes to the extraordinary lengths of taking him to a Christian orphanage. Meanwhile, at every seance where she appears, the dead Panderi continues to assert her loyalty to her husband's lineage and she finally persuades her younger sister to marry the husband in her stead. The interpretation of her death gives expression to conflicting views of her marriage. Whereas in the early stages it seems as if her family's view of the marriage will prevail, by the end the husband is able to see Panderi's death as an act of self-sacrifice and the supreme expression of her love.

A summary of shamanic procedure

COMBING THE HAIR OF THE WOMAN AT THE BOTTOM OF THE SEA

The father of the sea spirit Takanakapsaluk cruelly cut off her fingers, which turned into the different species of sea creatures on which the people depend. So it is only as a result of her suffering that humans can live and she may grant them animals or withhold them at will. When there is an incurable sickness, a hunter is particularly unsuccessful, or an entire village is threatened by famine, a shaman may be employed to descend to the seabed. He sits behind a curtain and after elaborate preparations calls his helpers, saying again and again, "The way is made ready for me, the way opens before me!" while the audience replies, "Let it be so!" Finally, from behind the curtain the shaman cries, "Halala - he - he - he, halala - he - he!" Then, as he drops down a tube which leads straight to the bottom of the sea, his voice can be heard receding ever further into the distance until it is lost altogether.

During the shaman's absence, the audience sits in the darkened house and hears the sighing and groaning of people who lived in the past. As soon as the shaman reaches the seabed, he has to dodge three deadly stones which churn around leaving hardly any room to pass. The entrance tunnel to the sea spirit's house is guarded by a fierce dog over which the shaman must step; he is also threatened by her father. He enters the house and finds Takanakapsaluk with her lamp and a great pool of sea creatures beside her, all puffing and blowing. As a sign of her anger, she is sitting with her back to the lamp and the pool. Her hair is filthy and uncombed and hangs over her eyes so that she cannot see. The dirt on her hair and body represents the sins and misdeeds of humans. The shaman turns her gently towards the lamp and the animals and combs her hair, for she has no fingers and is unable to do this for herself. Then he tells her, "Those above can no longer help the seals up by grasping their foreflippers," and she answers, "The secret miscarriages of the women and breaches of taboo in eating boiled meat bar the way for the animals." When the shaman has mollified her, Takanakapsaluk releases the

The sea spirit being cleansed (top), and releasing her animals (above).

animals and they are carried out by a torrent into the sea, to be available again to hunters.

Now the shaman returns. He can be heard a long way off returning through the tube which his helper spirits have kept open, and with one last "Plu - a - he -he" he shoots up into his place behind the curtain. After a silence he says, "Words will arise" and, one after another, people start to confess their misdeeds, often bringing out secrets which were quite unsuspected even in a small community living at close quarters. In particular, many women confess to having concealed miscarriages. After a miscarriage has taken place, all soft skins and furs belonging to everyone inside the house must be thrown away. This is such a serious loss that a woman may try to conceal any miscarriage or irregular bleeding. By the end of the seance there is such a mood of optimism that people may even feel grateful to the woman who caused the problem.

The diagram on the right represents a typical pattern of shamanic action, leading from a problem through a struggle to a resolution. The initial problem may be a single illness, an epidemic, or a life-threatening economic crisis such as crop failure or a shortage of animals. Given that there are intimate causal connections between any human actions

An Inuit whale figure attached to the bow of a hunting canoe in order to attract and pacify the spirits of the whales.

and the behaviour of the surrounding environment, these afflictions may well be a consequence of incorrect human behaviour such as a breach of taboo.

The cosmos must therefore be healed along with the humans, and it is the cosmos which provides the arena for action. At the same time, the cosmos also represents the human community or even the single person, as can be seen most intensely from a gynaecological expedition of the shaman's helper spirits into the patient's womb (see pp.158–9). Against this cosmic background, the object of the shaman's attention is the community or the person: the person's soul may have been abducted, or the community risks starvation. The drama is acted out simultaneously in physical, psychological and sociological idioms, all of which are encompassed in a religious attitude.

The shaman is able to act because of a relationship with spirits which gives him or her efficacy at the point in the spirit realm which is causing the problem. The shaman is qualified through initiation, repeated practice and public approval of his or her performances. The shaman is able to summon reliable helper spirits and overcome or tame hostile ones, because he or she has suf-

fered in a comparable way, for example by dying and then being resurrected.

The action taken by the shaman brings his or her qualification into the cosmic arena, through the technique of trance which makes possible the journey to the realm of the spirits. The centrepiece and turning point of the rite is the encounter between the shaman and the spirit who has power over the client. This may take the form of a physical battle between warriors, a tender coaxing between hunter and animal, a negotiation between business partners, a debate between a cunning opponent and an even more ingenious shaman, or a plea for mercy from a supplicant to a mighty lord. Whichever form this encounter takes, the shaman must prevail if the problem is to be resolved. The opposing spirit must be defeated, outwitted, won over, led to a compromise or made merciful. This is an opposition, maybe in the form of a literal dialogue, between the wrong way things are at the moment and the right way the community wishes them to be in the future. It is here that the rite's full implications are acted out most explicitly on every available level – in music, dancing and words. The shaman may also extract a harmful object from the patient's body, thereby removing an illness physically. There may be a catharsis, as people purge their "uncleanness" through public confession and repair their poisoned social relations. In a way which is by no means "merely" symbolic, the personal and social reality of the various participants will have been changed for the better.

Summary of Shamanic Procedure

Problem

- person ill
- crops fail
- animals escape
- community starving

Spirits as Cause and Cosmos as Arena of Action

- soul has been abducted
- community is impure
- foreign body has entered patient

Shaman as Agent of Cure

- summons reliable helper spirits
- defeats hostile spirits
- dies and is reborn

By Means of Extraordinary Knowledge and Power

- can journey across the Cosmos
- extract foreign body
- cleanse impurities

Decisive Action: Struggle

- physical battle
- cunning debate
- pleading supplication with spirit causing problem

Resolution

- Shaman prevails
- uncooperative spirit is sent back where it came from, dismissed into thin air, shut up in a pot, forced to agree to a compromise

Understanding Shamans

At first sight, the shaman's actions seem incompatible with the generally accepted worldview of industrial society. Shamanic thought conflicts with the "rational" and mechanistic models of cause and effect which operate in mainstream science. Yet some sciences seem quite open to unconventional ideas at their frontiers, and privately a lot of individuals are willing to believe in spirits. The main challenge that shamanism poses to modern ideas is perhaps a social and political one. Shamanism offers a worldview in which humans must use their environment not by dominating it but through a precarious and hard-won compromise, and at the price of constant attention and respect.

In a world in which most people's lives are becoming ever more depersonalized, a glimpse into shamanic society offers a view of relationships between humans based on the intimacy of the small-scale community which is fast disappearing. The neo-shamanic movements in big cities must work against this background and it remains to be seen whether shamanic ideas will be able to serve the needs of modern people in their increasingly fragmented and rootless society.

A self-portrait by a non-shaman who is suffering a pathological hallucination. The imagery of being devoured is similar to that employed by many shamans to describe their initiation.

Early impressions

Most shamans have not possessed a written tradition, and so the descriptions of them that survive have been written by outsiders. Because there can be no such thing as a neutral, objective description, these outsiders saw the shaman largely in terms of their own likes and dislikes. The people who were responsible for the early accounts of the shaman were representatives of more organized world religions, and were often also associated with colonial invasion and administration.

The Spanish Catholic priests who accompanied the conquistadors to the Caribbean and South America after 1492 found Indians who freely admitted that they were under the spell of spirits who incited them to warfare, cannibalism and intoxication. These spirits appeared to them as monsters with fangs, glowing eyes and roaring voices. The early, zealous, Catholic priests had no difficulty in recognizing these spirits as manifestations of their Christian Devil. This pattern of summoning devils and asking them not only to forecast the future, but also grant prestige or kill enemies, corresponded closely to the widespread European imagery of witchcraft. It was also accompanied by similar forms of possession, as well as

Toornaarsuk, a fierce but helpful spirit from Greenland, portrayed by early missionaries as the Devil.

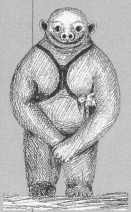

Figures of missionaries carved in the 18th century, probably by the Haida of the northwest coast of America.

ghosts and other frightening and ungodly phenomena. A state of trance, while under the influence of hallucinogenic plants, was interpreted as "talking with the devil", a view that contributed heavily to the brutal and tragic nature of European domination in that region.

The word "shaman" was introduced from Siberia into Russian literature in the less fanatical 17th century by the Russian Orthodox priest Avvakum. He saw the shaman as a religious figure, but one who serves the Devil rather than God. During the following century the administrators, traders and scholars who travelled in Siberia thought of shamans mainly as quacks or charlatans, although they were also seen by scholars as relics of an archaic form of religion (see pp.28–9). By the late 19th century, a view had evolved of the shaman as a special kind of mad person (see pp.138–41).

It was not only the many different Christian traditions and European administrations which interpreted the shaman in their own ways. Buddhist, Hindu and Taoist civilizations all encountered shamans and responded with various strategies of persecution, assimilation or co-existence (see pp.38–41 and pp.132–5).

ABOVE *The shamans or* piaches *of the Orinoco river are shown in a print from 1781 curing the tobacco and* maraka *used in their rituals.*

LEFT *In the 17th and 18th centuries, Siberian shamans were depicted in engravings as savage and animal-like but worthy of awe and respect because they were powerful magicians.*

AN ORACLE OF THE DEVIL

A ceremony involving a South American shaman who has taken hallucinogenic snuff is described by the Spaniard, Oviedo: "They worship the devil in diverse forms and images ... They make a demon they call *cemi*, as ugly and frightful as the Catholics represent him at the feet of St Michael or St Bartholomew; but not bound in chains, but revered: sometimes as if sitting in judgement ... These infernal images they had in their houses in specially assigned and dark places and spots that were reserved for their worship ... And inside there was an old Indian who answered them according to their expectations ... and it is to be thought that the devil entered into him and spoke through him as though through his minister ... These old men they greatly revered ... and without the devil's considered opinion ... they did not undertake or carry out anything that might be of importance."

THE SHRIEK OF A DEMON IN MEDIEVAL MONGOLIA

In the early 14th century, Franciscan friars in Mongolia would "think nothing of expelling demons from the possessed, as they would expel a dog from a house". They would take the "idols" (*ongons* or spirit-dolls) of the possessed person and carry them to the fire, but the idols would leap out of the fire again. "Because of this the brothers then take holy water which they throw into the fire. The demon flees from the fire and the idols are burnt up. Then the demon in the air shrieks, 'See, see how I am driven forth from my dwelling-place!' "

Shamanism in the history of religion

The idea that the shaman is a surviving archaic religious figure is common to most outsiders' interpretations, whether positive or negative. Eliade's book, *Shamanism*, probably the greatest single work on the subject, is subtitled "archaic techniques of ecstasy". According to Eliade, "[The] dialectic of the sacred tends indefinitely to repeat a series of archetypes, so that a hierophany [a manifestation of the sacred] realized at a certain 'historical moment' is structurally equivalent to a hierophany a thousand years earlier or later [...] In the most elementary hierophany everything is declared. The manifestation of the sacred in a stone or a tree is neither less mysterious nor less noble than its manifestation in a 'god'. The process of sacralizing reality is the

A Buddhist craftsman finishes off a demon figure before a procession in Sri Lanka.

The grave of a northern American Kwakiutl may combine Christian imagery with shamanic emblems, such as the whale.

same; the forms taken by the process in man's religious consciousness differ."

Western scholars have long been fascinated with questions of the ultimate origin of religion. In the 19th century, Tylor claimed that the idea of the soul, and hence religion itself, arose from people's experience of wandering while dreaming. At the turn of the century

the sociologist Durkheim argued, largely from his studies of Australian Aboriginal religion, that the origins of supernatural beings lay in a projection of society and that in religion society was in fact worshipping itself.

Palaeolithic discoveries in the 20th century (see pp.28–9) opened the way for interpretations that made the shaman the key figure in the quest for the origins of religion. La Barre argues that all our knowledge of the supernatural or the divine comes from shamans and similar visionaries. Since it is shamans who make the soul-journeys to the realms of supernatural beings, it must be they who gave the world its generally accepted ideas about the cosmos, heaven and hell. Priests merely represent a "routinization" of the shamanic role, since they no longer have the necessary visions themselves. Even the gods are former, early shamans who have grown greater since their deaths. While Eliade would not have agreed with all of this argument, he was concerned to distinguish pure forms of shamanism from degraded ones. In pure forms, the shaman attains "ecstasy" by spiritual means alone, whereas degraded forms include those in which the shaman relies on hallucinogenic chemistry for assistance. Such a viewpoint reduces Eliade to tracing shamanic strands through the regions of the world and evaluating them for authenticity, rather than seeing how they are actually used and felt by people who also live with other religions as part of their lives. North and South American Indian religion is pervaded with both Protestant and Catholic Christianity, and even the political rebellions against the white man have often taken the form of movements in search of a biblical kind of Messiah. The shamanism of the tribal Sora is in some ways very close to the worship of ancestors and village gods among their

A Hindu sadhu or holy man undertakes a trek to a sacred cave in Kashmir. His trident is used to sanctify the fire he builds at each stop on the way.

Hindu neighbours. Both place great emphasis on spirits and blood sacrifice, in contrast to the psychic restraint and vegetarianism of Brahmin forms of Hinduism. The forms of Buddhism adopted by converts in Western coun-

The Sufi dervishes of Turkey attain states of non-shamanic ecstasy through ritual recitation and physical exertions, such as whirling.

tries are almost nowhere to be found in Asia, where Buddhism is always entwined in the cult of gods and spirits. A shaman book which was written by a Manchu shaman in 1843 shows a mixture of Manchu shamanic spirits, the Buddha, the classical Chinese polarity of yin and yang, and the Emperor of Water Dragons. When a Sri Lankan Buddhist wants to exorcize a patient, he himself is possessed by the demon, although, somewhat like the shaman, the exorcist retains a measure of control over himself. Accompanied by the loud, rapid beat of drums, the exorcist breathes in demon-incense, gives a loud roar and rushes out into a ceremonial square, shaking violently. Later he will go to a cemetery and leave his demonic pollution there.

The shamanic experience has implications for various approaches to religion. The phenomenology of religion is

Possession is in some ways the opposite of shamanism, since the possessed person has no power over the spirit. Here, an old nun casts devils out of a young woman who is possessed. Bystanders hold cloths (above left) or hands (left) over their mouths to avoid breathing in the devils. The pictures were taken in Russia in the early days of Perestroika.

concerned with the forms in which the divine or spiritual manifests itself to us, and here shamans provide an experience that is extremely direct as well as relatively uncluttered by dogma. The complementary approach, through theology, is concerned with traditions of interpreting a given body of religious knowledge which is based on such manifestations. The understanding of the Christian concept of revelation can be greatly helped by study of the shamanic experience of spirit.

However, while prophets and other mystics with a direct experience of god are often crucial in the early stages of a world religion, in later stages they can present a dangerous challenge to established authority. The typical shamanic claim to incarnate or become a spiritual being can appear blasphemous, a view which is strengthened under monotheism. The Christian Church in later centuries, for example, has tended to suppress, marginalize or absorb this kind of mysticism. This authoritarian religious attitude is echoed even in modern psychological interpretations of shamanism, in which the shaman is a wild, mentally undisciplined person suffering from a nervous pathology, in contrast to specialists in more "disciplined" practices like meditation, contemplation or science.

SHAMANS VERSUS BUDDHISTS IN MONGOLIA

The 13th century was a time of rapid change in Central Asia. The Mongol chief Genghis Khan lived in the early 1200s in an old tribal world with clan shamans. This was no longer appropriate for the expanded international horizons of his successor Kublai Khan. As a boy in the 1220s, Kublai began to have daily discussions with a Tibetan lama whom he later made head of a new, institutionalized Mongolian Buddhist religion in 1264. Kublai himself adopted the Sanskrit title Chakravarti and declared himself to be a reincarnation of the former kings of Tibet and India. Mongolian Buddhism faded out with the decline of the Mongol empire, but it was reintroduced in the 17th century by Lamaist missionaries who persecuted the shamans to such an extent that Buddhism has remained the religion of Mongolia ever since. It has even survived through the more intense Communist persecution of the present century. While Lamaism was called the yellow faith, named after the Tibetan Yellow Hat sect, Mongolian

shamanism was called the "black faith". The lamas called shamanism the "old wrong way of seeing things", but as in Tibet and elsewhere, shamanic and Buddhist ideas and practices in fact became closely intertwined, so that they amounted to components in one wider religious system.

Some outlying areas of Mongol culture never adopted Buddhism. Among the Mongolian-speaking western Buryats near Lake Baikal in Siberia, a temple was built in 1840 and fourteen lamas installed. The local, shamanist population pointed out that the head lama was keeping concubines. He was replaced by a local man called Samsonov who had a wife and children and knew nothing about Buddhism. Samsonov set up *yurts* (tents) and outhouses for his collection of shamanist dolls (*ongons*). Samsonov's son tried to suppress shamanism but the local villagers thought that the idea of gaining religious merit by handing over their wealth to the lamas was a waste of resources. To escape his clutches, many joined the Orthodox Church and the shrines inside their *yurts* now contained *ongons* side by side with icons of St Nicholas.

Mongolian Buddhists at prayer. Buddhism absorbed many features of shamanism.

Communist regimes

Siberian graves had shamanic devices, such as the skins of sacrificed reindeer, even under Communism.

The Communist regimes of the 20th century covered much of the heartland of Asian shamanism, which was persecuted along with the region's many other religions. Since there were no shamanist churches or temples to pull down, persecution was aimed directly at the shamans themselves. In Siberia they were considered to be local leaders, class enemies hostile to the Soviet regime and were often sentenced to exile and sometimes dropped out of helicopters and challenged to fly. At the same time, the Marxist doctrine of the historical evolution of society saw them as the most primitive form of religious specialist and this combined with an existing scholarly fascination to produce a very

A Siberian shaman's grave.

detailed documentation of the rites and beliefs of the disappearing shamans.

In China, shamanism was widespread among the numerous minority peoples of Central Asia and here too it was suppressed along with other religions. Shamanism was considered "feudal superstition" fostered by fake healers who exploited their fellow-villagers for their own self-interest. Unlike the Soviet Union, there has been very little research into shamanism during most of the Communist period and much less is known about the recent situation there. In both Russia and China there is now a great interest in old shamanic traditions, and in Russia attempts are being made to revive some of them.

A thread from the roof links the sky and the earth. The thread is then burned to keep the patient's soul on earth.

THE DRUMS WHICH BELONGED TO THE MAN FROM THE KGB

Some time after the terrors of Stalin's reign, a Russian anthropologist travelling in Siberia was helped by some local people. When he offered to repay their help, he was told, "We don't want anything in return, we'd just like to look at the collection of shamans' drums which we know you've got." The Siberians went to the man's apartment in the city and looked at his private collection. One of them picked out just two of the drums and said, "You are a good man and these two drums are all right so long as they remain in your possession. But if they ever pass into anyone else's hands, something terrible could happen." The collector was astonished, because he knew that these two drums had a sinister history. They had belonged to a KGB officer who had worked in a remote area of Siberia. This officer had been in the habit of visiting small settlements pretending to be ill and asking for the local shaman. When the shaman appeared ready to help him, the officer would lead him to a lonely place and shoot him. He would then take the drums of the shamans he had shot as trophies. It seems that many years later something of this dark history was communicated to the native man.

THE SHAMAN AND THE POLICE CHIEF

The story is told of how a Soviet police chief threatened an old Yakut shaman with his revolver. The shaman told him gently, "My son, don't do that, you'll hurt yourself." Somehow, the policeman shot off his own thumb. He was furious and blamed the shaman, who was jailed, but mysteriously escaped and came walking in through the door of the police station. He was put in ever more tightly guarded cells, but each time he escaped, only to turn himself in. Finally he was sentenced to hard labour in a remote forest, cutting down a grove of trees and chopping them up for firewood. An inspection team visited him in the summer and were astonished to see his axe flying magically around the clearing, felling trees and stacking the logs up neatly. At the beginning of winter the authorities came to collect the firewood, but the shaman had disappeared and so had the stacks of logs. They had joined themselves up into living trees.

The Yakut anthropologist and poet Kulakovsky wrote a long poem called *The Shaman's Dream* in which he predicted the destruction of the Yakut people under Soviet rule and urged resistance to the last man. The first President of the Soviet Republic of Yakutia was Platon Sleptsov, who was also a poet and a great singer of traditional Yakut heroic epic songs. He adopted the pen-name of Oyunsky, meaning "Son of the Shaman".

A Russian anti-shaman poster.

Are shamans mentally ill?

It was from the turn of the 20th century that scholars and investigators began to emphasize the psychopathology, "hysteria" or "neurosis" of the shaman. These views were largely based on the particularly violent and alarming performances of the Siberian shamans. Lommel's view in the 1960s of the palaeolithic shaman's mental disorder as a necessary stimulus to artistic creativity (see pp.28–9) was a significant step on the road that leads through the hippy era to the New Age, where the shaman is seen as perhaps the most sane of people. The strange behaviour of shamans while in a state of trance is now generally thought to lie within the range of "normal" human behaviour, and may even be regarded as a universal psychobiological talent. The pathological, ineffectually "fantasy-prone" shaman of the past has become today's creative imaginer. This turnaround of opinion was helped in the 1960s by the widespread experimentation with different forms of psychedelic drugs.

Perhaps the closest parallel to shamanic "madness" is in the clinical condition of schizophrenia. A schizophrenic episode can plunge a person into terrors comparable to the Siberian shaman's initiation vision, as his or her personality disintegrates in the same way. However, both psychologically and socially, the differences are great. Where the shaman's concentration is increased, that of the schizophrenic is scattered; where the shaman retains a far-reaching control of his or her own state of mind, schizophrenia entails a loss of this control; and where the shaman's experience is always brought back to society and shared for society's benefit, the schizophrenic is trapped inside a private experience, almost to the point of autism.

The common schizophrenic hallucination of oral-genital devouring on the right can be compared to an Inuit shaman's drawing of his helper spirit, above. Soon after the shaman lost his parents, this spirit came to him and said, "You must not be afraid of me for I too struggle with sad thoughts."

Outside trance, the shaman is usually a normal, even ordinary person. As with other kinds of creative personalities, some seem excitable or strange while others are sturdy and competent members of their communities. The existence of the difficult and temperamental Beethoven does not preclude – or explain – the creativity of a deeply steady personality like Bach. The surest argument for seeing shamans as being basically psychologically sound is that the community could not otherwise entrust them with the protection of its own mental health and livelihood.

The shaman's mental strength comes from an expanded experience of mental disturbance. The initiation is a controlled disintegration which is always followed by a reintegration into someone more powerful and more whole. The shamanic personality is moulded

This vision of "silent horribleness" appeared to an Inuit shaman who was so violently scared that he ran before trying to enlist it as a helper.

by the culture, and shamans are "mad" by courtesy of the culture and on the terms of that culture. It is ultimately society which distinguishes between the behaviour of the shaman and that of the schizophrenic or psychotic. One becomes a hero, the other a hospital patient. The shaman lives on the brink of the abyss but has the means to avoid falling in.

Flashing lights, bright colours and fireworks displays – represented here in a drawing by a schizophrenic – are a common early stage in visual hallucination.

A schizophrenic's drawing of a posture which represents an aspect of his own character. It is similar to Arctic shamans' drawings which represent their spiritual rather than their physical state.

THE AGE OF SHAMANIC INSANITY

The Russian anthropologist Basilov summarizes Russian literature from the early 20th century on the shaman's mental state: "In the 19th century the shaman's wild antics were given a straightforward explanation. Shamans were cunning charlatans who pretended to be possessed by 'demons' in order to deceive their naive fellow-tribespeople. At the beginning of our century a different opinion arose: shamans were people of a disordered mind, neurotics. While this suggestion was still very tentative in Mikhailovsky in 1892, by 1905 Kharuzin was proposing 'to recognize that all true shamans are above all neurotic persons'. Bogoraz claimed in 1910 that among the shamans known to him, 'many were almost hysterical and some were literally half-insane.

Shamanism is a form of religion created through the selection of the most nervously unstable persons.' In 1929 Ksenofontov published *The Cult of Madness in Ural-Altaic Shamanism* while Zelenin wrote in 1935 that it was impossible for a mentally healthy person to become a shaman at all."

This view was no more extreme than what was being written in western Europe and North America. In 1939 Ohlmarks connected the "arctic hysteria" of Siberian and Eskimo peoples with the long winter nights and lack of vitamins, while other reseachers found similar hysterias throughout the tropics. Until his recent death the great psychoanalytic anthropologist Devereux maintained that Mohave shamans were mentally ill and he wrote books with chapter headings such as, "Insanity due to dreaming of an insane deity".

PSYCHOANALYSIS AND THE
REGRESSIVE SHAMAN

To the Freudian psychoanalyst the echoes in every shamanic journey of the trauma of initiation suggest a neurotic or compulsive repetition. A fuller version of the story of the Yakut shaman who rescues a woman from the raven-headed people in the sky (see p.101) has been analysed by the psychoanalyst Ducey. The rescue is told not from the position of the woman saved, nor even from that of the shaman who did the rescuing, but from the perspective of a novice shaman who watches the action while he is lying in a nest on the ninth branch of the world tree, being breast-fed by a white reindeer. The shaman who rescues the woman is older than the novice and was nursed on the same tree. But he was nursed only on the eighth branch and is later surpassed and killed by the younger shaman.

Ducey interprets the story as an oedipal conflict between the young shaman and a father figure. The young shaman's attachment to his mother is represented both by the suckling and by the narrow entrance to the sky which suggests that the whole incident takes place inside the womb of the novice's mother. The appearance of the older shaman's head through this narrow opening represents the father's penis during intercourse with the mother in whose womb the young shaman is growing. The son is jealous of this intimacy but can do nothing about it on the first two occasions. The third time, the intruder is repelled at the threshold by firebrands.

This excursion into the shaman's psychology does not lead Ducey to a pathological assessment. He concludes that the story is an allegory of growing up in which the son replaces the father, and that the initiation enables the child to emerge from the "pre-oedipal" world of autistic fantasy (breastfeeding) and enter the "oedipal" realm of shared cultural fantasies. The story allows these fantasies to be fulfilled, but in a setting of shared cultural experience. The implication of his analysis seems to be that through his initiation the shaman lives out the fantasy on behalf of the wider society.

A non-shaman's painting of his reawakened childhood memory of his melancholic mother.

Do shamans really heal?

However outsiders may understand the shaman's own mental state, shamanic societies see a continuity between this and the state of the patient and of society as a whole. Like the shaman's initiation, the patients' "illnesses" too are in fact episodes in their overall personal development. The question "Does the shaman heal?" is only a smaller part of the question "Is any of this real?" In both cases, the answer must move away from narrow concepts of experimental scientific validation towards understanding different peoples' assumptions about the nature of reality. Procedures

ABOVE *A Wana shaman of Indonesia carries his patient's life contained in a betel-leaf offering and carefully wrapped up in a cloth tied around his back. He is taking it in a canoe up to Pue, the Owner in the sky.*

LEFT *A shaman of the Sitka-Quan Indians in Alaska treats a bewitched patient, while wearing a head-dress and a special ceremonial mask called a tolu-ga. With one hand he shakes a spirit-rattle and with the other he holds a medicinal ivory necklace to the patient's chest.*

like "reality testing" do not test reality but test new material against a pre-conceived notion of reality. Shamanic cultures have particular assumptions about what exists (ontology) and how things happen (causality). If one shares these assumptions, then the possibility of effective shamanic action follows.

Conventional Western medicine also works in this way. There is a great deal of ritual, awe and status involved in most people's consultations with a doctor, and the "placebo effect" shows that people given a dummy pill often respond to it as well as if it contained an active medicine. In most situations where shamans are available, patients combine shamanic treatment with hospital medicine in subtle and complex ways. Conventional medicine in turn is increasingly influenced by shamanic attitudes, especially where the focus is on fostering a good relationship between doctor and patient. The parallels are closest in psychotherapy and also where healing involves a social context, as in group therapy. These approaches emphasize the need to understand the world and one's own position in it. The ritual works because it expresses needs and feelings, but it also changes the patient's health by altering perception (see pp.156–8). There may be physiological effects but these are not the only proof of efficacy, just as the physiological symptoms alone are not the illness itself.

A Sora shaman enhances his prestige by using the stethoscope of a medical doctor (right) and the herbal tonics of a Hindu Ayervedic physician (below).

At a funeral among the Sora, a shaman enters a trance surrounded by assistants and mourners.

THE SLOW, PAINFUL PROCESS OF SHAMANIC HEALING

A little girl who died recently has returned to speak with her young mother. Her mother is too overcome with grief to respond and the talking is done on her behalf by an older woman, the child's aunt. The dialogue takes place during a Sora shaman's trance just a few months after the little girl died. The living regard her with mixed feelings of tenderness but also fear that she may pass on her illness to others, as the recently dead always do among the Sora.

Dead little girl: [arriving from the Underworld, faintly] Mother, where are my nose-rings?
Living Aunt: [answering for the girl's mother] They must have burned up in the pyre, darling, we looked but couldn't find them. I don't know whether they jumped to one side or what.
Little girl: [petulantly] Why aren't you showing me my nose-rings?
Aunt: They were so tiny. If I'd found them of course I'd show them to you. *[A pause; the aunt continues:]* Oh my love, my darling, don't

cause your own illness in others. Can you say that your mother and father didn't sacrifice for you? They didn't turn their backs or refuse to help you, did they? Think of all those pigs, all those chickens, goats, buffaloes, my lovely child. Didn't your father say, "Let's light a fire, let her stay at home and not go out to work, look at her, she's already got the face of an old woman," didn't he say that? ... What? Your two gold necklaces aren't here. Your brother's wearing them now....
Little girl: [addressing herself to her silent mother, and crying] Mother, you were horrid to me, you scolded me, you called me Scar-Girl, you called me Leper-Girl, you said, "You're a big girl now, why should I feed you when you sit around doing nothing?"
Aunt: She didn't mean it, she couldn't help saying it: after all, you were growing up and there were such a lot of chores to do.
Little girl: [sulkily] I want my necklaces ... I used to hobble round bent double, I couldn't stand up straight ... *[Unreasonable childish tone:]* Why can't I have my nose-rings? I have to go digging, shovelling and levelling earth *[in the Underworld]*, all without my nose-rings.

My mother gave it to me in her womb, it's in her family. I came out in scars all over, my fingers started dropping off. That illness was passed on to me, that's how I got ill.
Aunt: Then don't you pass it on, don't you give it to your mother and little sisters!
Little girl: If I grab them I grab them, if I touch them I touch them, if I pass it on I pass it on: that's how it goes.
Aunt: Your cough, your choking, your scars, your wounds, don't pass them on ...
Little girl: My Mummy doesn't care enough about me *[returns to the Underworld]*.

The effect on the girl's mother is at first completely devastating, because the little girl's reproaches exactly mirror what we might call the mother's own self-reproach. It is in the evolution of this dialogue over the course of the next few years that the healing power of Sora shamanism lies. The little girl will gradually come round to saying that her mother was a good mother and that no grudges remain. Because these early, cruel conversations so closely match the feelings of the mourners, the later modification will be equally convincing. It will also be comforting, as the girl becomes disinclined to pass her illness on to her living relatives and turns into a supporting and protective spirit instead.

THE HEALING POWER OF DIALOGUE

Shamanic healing may involve a dialogue between the patient and someone else, either the shaman or a spirit. This is carried to extraordinary lengths in Sora shamanism but is also present in psychoanalysis, which is likewise a "talking cure". A Sora patient talks to the dead through a specialist, while a psychoanalyst's patient talks to the specialist about other, absent personalities in the patient's life.

The diagram shows the logical relations between these two approaches and clinical psychiatry. From left to right, it depicts a progressive separation of the body from the soul or mind and the emergence of the category "medicine" as a readiness to treat the body on its own. At each stage, what is at issue is not the nature of reality, but the appropriateness of technique. What is trimmed off at each stage is not simply a spiritual aspect of the patient. The inclusion of the soul means not just that the body is seen as related to it, but also that the person is seen in relation to other persons. So what is trimmed off is a layer of integration in the social dimension of the whole encounter – that is, the degree of dialogue involved. As a form of psychotherapy, Sora shamanism is based on a dialogue which takes place between the mourner and the person on whom his or her attention is focused. Psychoanalysis is likewise based on dialogue, but the other speaker is absent and the analyst plays the role of a pale substitute. Clinical psychiatry, in its use of tranquillizers and shock therapy, does not use dialogue as a therapeutic technique.

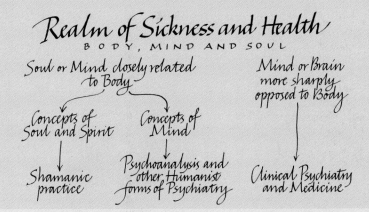

Realm of Sickness and Health
BODY, MIND AND SOUL

Soul or Mind closely related to Body

Mind or Brain more sharply opposed to Body

Concepts of Soul and Spirit

Concepts of Mind

Shamanic practice

Psychoanalysis and other Humanist forms of Psychiatry

Clinical Psychiatry and Medicine

Kinds of consciousness

The 1960s' emphasis on psychedelic drugs has been largely superseded by a much wider interest in the whole range of what are now called "altered states of consciousness" or ASC. Psychologists are not so concerned with the question of the reality of spirits or of their social context. Instead, they tend to look for the universal human psychobiological potentials which are supposedly culture-free and which can be reproduced and studied under laboratory conditions. This research uses neurophysiology (the study of the nervous system) – especially the relationship between drum rhythms and brain-waves – and chemistry, through the study of opiate-like compounds called endorphins. New Age and neo-shamanist practitioners share this commitment to the idea of states of consciousness that are independent of cultures, for although they find some ethnography fascinating and moving, they do not wish to be closely tied to all its specific features.

Some authors speak of a general religious state of consciousness or of a trance state which encompasses both shamanism and possession. Others identify a distinctive shamanic state of trance or ecstasy based on the shaman's experience of soul flight. Although some speak of a single "shamanic state of consciousness", it seems increasingly likely that there are many.

A broader and more far-reaching approach is offered by Walsh, who disputes the belief that shamans, yogis and Buddhists all "access" the same state of consciousness. He argues that just as shamanic consciousness was previously confused with pathological states like schizophrenia, it is now confused with meditative and yogic states. Even this shamanic consciousness must vary between the clear light of an exhilarating journey to the sky and a terrifying journey to murky worlds below the earth. Biochemical and physiological measurements, says Walsh, are not needed if we concentrate on what people say they experience, an approach

Two Palawan shamans from Indonesia, in a state of trance and displaying their offerings for the spirits. Their faces are covered with scarves in order to simulate blindness and activate their second sight.

A drawing of a model made by an experimental subject only 20 minutes after taking a dose of LSD.

After an hour and 25 minutes the subject sees the model clearly, but his hands are making sweeping movements.

Two hours 30 minutes: the subject feels that his consciousness resides in his drawing hand.

Shortly after the previous drawing, the subject feels unable to draw the model as he sees him.

Shortly after the previous drawing, the subject feels he has captured a likeness in one sweep of his hand.

Two hours 45 minutes: everything is kaleidoscopic and mobile. The model's face has become diabolical.

Four hours 25 minutes: the world grows quieter.

Five hours 45 minutes: the world ebbs and flows.

Eight hours: the subject is confused and tired. He finds his own drawing "boring".

which for thousands of years has allowed mystics to classify states of consciousness with great precision in many different schools and practices.

Walsh characterizes the shamanic states of consciousness as being intensely concentrated. The shaman's experiences are coherent and highly organized according to the purpose of the journey and the symbolic imagery used in a given society. Walsh contrasts this with Patanjali's method of yoga and Buddhist *vipassana* insight meditation. The former is based on unwavering concentration on inner objects and the latter on a fluid attention to all objects. In their calmness, however, they both differ from shamanic consciousness, which is a highly aroused state as the shaman flies between worlds and battles with spirits. Although Walsh does not say this, such a comparison makes the shaman's degree of control appear only partial, as the relation with spirits is a tempestuous and stressful one.

Both traditional and psychological

K.A.

An entrail-robber spirit, which tries to make the shaman laugh. If he succeeds he kills the shaman.

ways of talking about consciousness use metaphors of space and maps. One current neo-shamanist project aims to map, literally, the realm of non-ordinary reality. But one can also see the shamanic journey's movement between locations as a metaphor for changes of consciousness which cannot be expressed in any other language.

ENDORPHINS AND ENDURANCE

While drumming and hallucinogenic plants provide an external trigger for psychic states, the question remains of how the body and the mind respond to them. During the 1970s, biologists reported that under certain kinds of stimulation the body produces its own substances, called endorphins, which are similar to morphine and reduce the body's sensitivity to pain by attaching themselves to

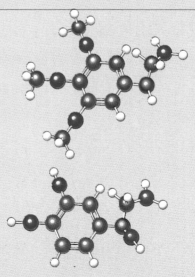

receptors on nerve cells. As well as analgesia they can induce euphoria, amnesia and altered states of consciousness. The role of endorphins in inducing shamanic states of consciousness and making possible feats of endurance remains obscure. They cannot explain the content or emotional tone of the shaman's experience.

The similar chemical structures of the peyote *hallucinogen (above), and* noradrenaline, *a natural brain hormone (below).*

The Zen garden of rocks and raked sand of the Ryoanji, in Kyoto, Japan.

ZEN AWARENESS

There are many states of human consciousness. The consciousness in Zen Buddhism is different from that in *vipassana* Buddhism:

In Zen, the way people should move towards perfect composure is to forget everything and to have nothing at all in their consciousness, no trace or shadow of their thinking. Then their minds will be able to see and feel things as they are. But if they try to stop their minds consciously, this will only give them another burden and they will become preoccupied with the need to stop their minds. There are different schools of Zen, according to whether composure is approached mainly through meditation or by contemplating *koans*, or paradoxical questions such as "What is the sound of one hand clapping?" or "What is the meaning of Mu [a nonsense sound]?"

A Zen master says: "Do not try to stop your mind, but leave everything as it is ... Things will come as they come and go as they go. Eventually your clear, empty mind will last fairly long."

INHIBITIONS

A shamanic state of consciousness can be reached and maintained only with difficulty. Chini, a young Korean candidate, has been suffering torment because she is destined to become a shaman and yet cannot act out the performance for her initiation. The gods have not yet empowered her to act as a shaman for clients. At a first ceremony she was cleansed of unwelcome ghosts; by the second one it is hoped that the spirits will give her the necessary powers. But at the ceremony, Chini cannot lose herself in the performance and give herself to the spirits. Her living teacher shouts instructions, "Jump and keep shouting out the spirits' commands," but Chini keeps lapsing into silence. A Buddhist sage, speaking through her mouth, explains that an intrusive spirit is blocking her and the spirits will not grant her the power without a further year's hard work. Chini keeps doing everything wrong and the more her teacher corrects her, the more she gets flustered and her mistakes increase. This obstructing spirit turns out to be Chini's own pockmarked sister, who was destined to become a shaman but who committed suicide instead. This dead sister casts an inhibition on Chini's ability to perform as a shaman, an inhibition which may be permanent.

New shamanic movements

The picture of the shaman as psychotic persists in some quarters even today, but it has largely been eclipsed by a new and more positive evaluation. Aldous Huxley experimented with mescalin in the early 1950s and the appreciation of shamanism has grown steadily since then both among academic specialists and in popular culture. From 1968, Castaneda's books on the Yaqui Indian teacher Don Juan became cult reading and posed a serious challenge to conventional frameworks of reality and ideas about its limits. The figure of the shaman is idealized in dissident psychiatry and many other quarters.

This groundswell has been reinforced by the collapse of European empires accompanied by a new hesitancy in Euro-American intellectual colonialism.

Western industrial culture has begun to suffer an increasing loss of confidence in Christianity and the scientific world-view. A similar disillusionment has taken place in the former Communist world. This process has led to a spiritual quest which has been met by diverse forms of religion such as charismatic churches, Buddhism or paganism. Among these, shamanism is seen as a non-institutionalized, undogmatic form of spirituality which offers considerable scope for personal creativity. Currently, "shamanism" is taken by young people as the ultimate form of individual freedom in electronic "techno" dancing, a far cry from the scholarly obscurity of early 20th-century shamanic studies.

From the 1970s, new shamanic movements have sprung up in the USA and

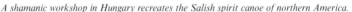

A shamanic workshop in Hungary recreates the Salish spirit canoe of northern America.

Europe. These combine the legacy of the drug culture of the 1960s with a long-standing interest in non-Western religions, current environmentalist movements, strands of the New Age movement and all the various forms of self-help and self-realization. Popular anthropology has also contributed, especially via the work of Castaneda. These movements take the strongest form of the view that shamanism is opposed to institutionalized religion and political systems and speak of a democratization of shamanism in which every person can be empowered to become their own shaman. They think of shamanism not so much as a religion but as a view of reality and an effective technique.

A spirit canoe, containing playful animal helpers, drawn by a Canadian shaman in 1972.

Teaching is carried out by various foundations and groups using weekend workshops and other courses with supporting literature and tapes. Neo-shamanists interpret the shamanic "altered state of consciousness" as a universal human potential which is only partially realized in any given traditional culture. For example, the Harner Method teaches a "core shamanism" which has been abstracted from several different cultures. The North American founder of this method, Michael Harner, has said that "many of these traditions have a lot of elements in them that are not really shamanic, but relate to the cultural configuration [and] have no relevance to us in our culture. I'm trying to understand the basic universals of shamanism and to present these bare bones to the people I teach [so that they can] integrate these things into their own lives."

However, this approach raises problems which are not easy to resolve. Traditional cultures form almost the entire history of shamanism and provide the basis for our knowledge about it, yet they contain integral elements which are incompatible with other New Age values such as vegetarianism, feminism or a desire to separate healing completely from sorcery. There is a risk that the new shamanists may create their own ideal image of shamanism and then judge traditional societies as failing to live up to this image.

Nepalese student shamans taking notes.

INDUSTRIAL POLLUTION:
THE SONG OF THE AIR

New movements combine shamanic themes with other major concerns of our age. They draw on the integrated world-view of traditional shamanism and link this to current environmental problems:

"We also spoke to the Air, this time I went up to my Power Place to the Dance Ground of the Winds. I danced a little there and, as I danced, the Airs sang to me.

The Airs you have poisoned
By your cars, your smoke,
your factories
And again the Spiral's turning
Poison Air and poison Water
Trees start dying in the forest
Poison Air, poison your
children
Harm the future of your
species

Dance the Spiral never ending
Dance the Air, the Earth, the
Water
By your dance you hope can
give us
Dance like trees, like birds,
like insects
Dance like flowers, like wind,
like spirits
Dance like fire the Spiral for
us
As we call you Spirit-Speaker
So we'll call you a Web
Healer
As you dance the Web
unending
Heal the sick parts of the
World.

The Airs spoke to me of my mission in this work, in this life. I was to help to heal the world itself. By my work, by my dance, I was to be a

A Nepalese Life Tree, on which the shaman experiences spiritual rebirth, reproduced in a wood in Hungary by neo-shamanists.

healer of the Web, an Earth shaman."

[Karen Kelly, from *I see with different eyes*, privately printed, Cambridge 1993.]

The involvement of the new movements in ecological matters has coincided with indigenous peoples' own demands to re-establish ancient relationships with their lands. When, in 1990, oil companies proposed to drill in caribou calving grounds, they were confronted by the Gwich'in people of Alaska and the Yukon. A Gwich'in-born speaker in the Yukon Legislature said, "Our people ... have lived with that herd for over 30,000 years. We have always been here. We cannot let that happen."

SHAMANIC COUNSELLING

"Shamanic counselling" is a term widely used in some New Age circles and elsewhere. In one well-established method the patient (here called a client) is invited to concentrate on a personal problem for which he or she would like to seek advice. The client is then helped to travel mentally to upper and lower worlds in "non-ordinary reality" and seek guidance from spirit beings encountered there. It is the client who makes this journey, rather than the specialist, and each client is encouraged to become his or her own shaman. The rationale for this is that in a "spiritual democracy" people should not need to seek spiritual authority from someone outside themselves, at least not in ordinary reality. The real counsellors are the spirit guides in non-ordinary reality. This technique was developed by an anthropologist who is familiar with shamanism worldwide. While travelling under the counsellor's guidance, the client is encouraged to use certain classic shamanic techniques such as acting out dialogues or mimed encounters with power animals and mythic personages. Although real drums are also used, the journey is often made to the sound of a tape-recorded drumbeat which the client hears through headphones. Apart from being better adapted to life in crowded apartments, this allows clients to narrate their experiences as they occur, so that they can later discuss them with the counsellor.

BACK TO THE PALAEOLITHIC WITH ACID-HOUSE RAVE

"Trance brings on a liberating state of consciousness," says Colin. " You get into contact with a space of inspiration and freedom. That makes people go out of their heads. After all these psychedelic experiences I know that somewhere inside there's a profound longing to get back to the palaeolithic states that we used to experience thousands of years ago. We're indebted to psychedelic plants for making the human group stick together and for an acute sense of the ecological link which unites us to the planet."

"All the raves today are a load of crap." The Shamen, professionals in tribalism, are fed up. "Too much hardcore, too much violence, too many machos!" In the past two years the rave movement has gone mad. The tempo has speeded up amazingly. "At 160 beats a minute, 180 beats a minute, you get tachycardia. The rhythm gets you down!" One curious thing: the rhythm began to go mad when the quality of the ecstasy went down. "The only stuff you find now is spiked with amphetamines and heroin. That has nothing to do with what we used to know."

[From an interview with the pop group The Shamen in the French magazine *Actuel*, Jan-Feb 1993, pp.64–5, translated by the author.]

Despite the claims of authorities, worried parents and even a number of users, the

Psychedelic lighting may induce a trance state.

designer drug ecstasy is not actually hallucinogenic. It does, however, stimulate a sustained condition of high excitement which allows the user to dance with greater vigour, for longer periods. This increased endurance is thought to give the lighting and the beat of the music more of an opportunity to induce a trance-like state in the dancer (see pp.78–81).

The cosmos within

In Chinese legend, the shamanically inspired trickster-figure of Monkey multiplies himself many-fold in order to defeat the White Bone Demon.

Shamanism is a chameleon-like phenomenon, reappearing across diverse regional traditions, in varied historical and political settings and co-existing, sometimes uneasily, with major world religions. Shamanic ideas lack the institutional framework and the centralization represented by a Pope or a Dalai Lama, or by the great temples of Hinduism. Being fluid and innovative, such ideas can be adapted to work in the remotest forest, in the court of the Chinese Emperor or even in a workshop in downtown San Francisco. For the shaman, any world can be the other world. In the depths of the Indian jungle, the other world is that of the bazaar with its bicycles and aeroplanes, while in Siberia and Amazonia it includes doctors from other planets.

Rather than looking for an institution we can call shamanism, our understanding should focus on the figure of the shaman. The shaman unites areas such as religion, psychology, medicine and theology which in Western life have become separate. Through his or her extraordinary individual experiences

A LANDSCAPE OF LEOPARDS OR A LANDSCAPE OF PSYCHOSIS?

A Sora landscape is rich in associations and imagery relating to the lives and the minds of its inhabitants. The village and surrounding rice fields at the bottom of the valley are the domain of ancestor spirits, who are mostly supportive and nourish their descendants by putting their own soul-force into their growing crops. The jungle on the steeper slopes is the domain of a number of spirits which reside in trees and rocks and attack the living in order to absorb them into themselves.

Each of these spirits represents a distinct form of death, so that someone killed by a leopard will join Leopard-Spirit and reside in that spirit's site. From there, the dead person will join other leopard victims to attack passers-by with actual leopards or by producing scratching and clawing symptoms. Much of Sora shamanism consists of talking to the dead and persuading them to become benign ancestors rather than representatives of hostile jungle spirits.

A Sora shaman's patients suffer from the effects of human consciousness stored in rocks and trees, rather than from disorders such as schizophrenia and psychosis. The psychiatrist's or psychoanalyst's patients live in an isolated world of personal symbolism which can be shared at best only with their doctor. By contrast, the Sora mental map is the same as that of the physical landscape over which groups of people walk, work and dispute every day of their lives. This is equally a map of the social order in the broadest sense. Dialogues with the dead bring together a crowd of people who all agree which spirits are where and who has been absorbed into each of them.

It is this common landscape that furnishes the means by which both personal experience and the social order are regulated and perpetuated. For the Western secular tradition generally, the structure of experience is based largely on the structure of the experiencing mind, with its various subdivisions into conscious and unconscious, or ego, id and superego. For the Sora, the mind is not subdivided but rather the structure of human experience is based on the structure of the outside world which the mind apprehends.

A Sora landscape. The small boy is a shaman's son, and already sees spirits all around him.

the shaman's means are psychological but the ends are sociological, to heal and maintain the community. Even the shaman's psychology is partly socially conditioned: there can be no state of mind without a history or without the surrounding politics and social structures with all their fault lines and contradictions. If it is true that shamans utilize a universal human potential, then the practice and the valuation of this potential is constantly changing.

Shamanism is not only a religion or a facet of religion, it is a very active and practical one. Although shamans are mystics and experience the basic patterns of the world and appreciate them for their own sake, everything a shaman does is ultimately directed towards regulating some aspect of the world on behalf of the community. The shaman's soul travels in order to rescue the souls of others, to fight demons and to obtain food and material resources. A little Sora girl's dreams are a private experience, but as she becomes a shaman she places her experience at the service of her public inside the formalized framework of ritual. In the Siberian shaman Dyukhade's initiatory vision (see pp.60–61), what the seven cliffs showed him was not simply how the world worked but how the cliffs served to furnish the basic materials for human technology.

Shamans and their clients often seem barely distinguishable, as the universal human capacity to dream is developed into a specialized technique of trance, or as the initiatory illness of the shaman provides a qualification to treat comparable illnesses in a patient. All members of the society share the same cosmos and landscape. In a shamanic culture, mapping one's mental state on to a geography of somewhere outside one-

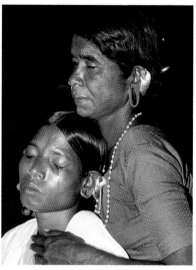

A new Sora shaman in her first trance, frightened and in tears, but comforted by an older woman.

self is not just the privilege of the shaman, but is a basic way of talking about one's emotions and social relationships. This may be a geography of the universe, or it may be a geography of the trees and bus-stops outside someone's house. The young Sora wife who died to save her baby (see p.124) perished as the direct result of walking past a certain spot on the path between two villages. But the connection which was made between herself and that location also summarized both sides of a debate about her love for her husband and gave a verdict on the validity of their marriage.

The Nepalese shaman, when he flies around the Kathmandu valley, reads the associations which are condensed and stored in the various locations he passes and thereby sees the various experiential dynamics embedded in a patient's condition. When he returns and presents this visionary knowledge to the patient, he is making explicit what the patient already knew, but only implicitly or "unconsciously". The patient's chaotic feelings are translated into images which can be visited, recounted and reflected upon in a clear, disciplined order that is like the mapped and ordered layout of geography itself.

BELOW *A Chinese acupuncture chart. Acupuncture is based on the idea that the principles of Yin (female and dark) and Yang (male and light) act in the human body as they do throughout the universe. An imbalance of Yin and Yang in the body blocks the flow of life-force, which can be released again by inserting pins in appropriate parts of the body.*

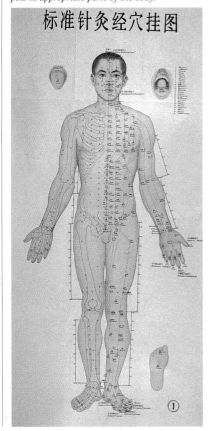

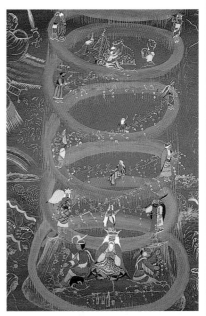

ABOVE *The blurring of the boundaries between the shaman and the cosmos can apply in both directions. In this painting by an ex-shaman from Peru, sublime masters of medicine descend down a spiral from heaven on to a* vegetalista.

This is symbolized by the locations in which the Nepalese shaman may come across the patient's lost soul, in crema-tion grounds and in swamps, cowering "above a great rock, above a great tree, above a great cliff, above a great scar in the earth, above a crevasse." In rescuing the soul, the shaman removes his patients from the psychic condition associated with these wild and wretched places and transfers them to a whole-some state. He leads the patient out of one metaphor, or state of mind, into another. This wildness has its uses, however. These sites and mental states are reminiscent of those which the shaman himself experienced during ini-tiation. Like the shaman, the patient is also undergoing a transformation. A sickness, once healed, can be given a positive interpretation: as an American Indian medicine-man said, "With white man's medicine, you only get back to the way you were before; with Indian medicine, you can get even better!"

The mind or spirit has extraordinary properties which for most people lie untapped. It is true that soul flight gives the shaman the power to see another reality, but over-emphasis on a trip of discovery can lead to a false sense of shamanhood. The shaman is dedicated to easing the difficulties of other people, and the torment of the shaman's initiation is also the pain of the community. The shaman's performance unites the inner and the outer worlds, the worlds of the individual and of society, the world contained in the mind or body and that of the cosmos beyond.

AN EMERGENCY EXPEDITION INTO THE WOMB

The shamanic cosmos is not only "out there" but is inside every one of us, and the shaman who journeys through the cosmos is also travelling through the community's own mental and physical space. Sometimes the correspondences go further than simply referring to the community's familiar landscape and the shamanic voyage takes place entirely inside a patient's body. Among the Cuna Indians of Panama, each part of the body has its own spirit or essence which symbolizes that organ's function. Childbirth takes place through an essence of the womb called Muu. In the following rite to induce labour, Muu is seen as the shaman's adversary but she is not so much an evil spirit as a bodily function which is not working as it should. The analogy between the patient's inner anatomy and the geography of the cosmos is made clear: "The inner white tissue extends to the bosom of the earth... Into the bosom of the earth her exudations gather into a pool, all like blood, all red."

The shaman sits under the sick woman's hammock and repeats at great length the steps by which the midwife sent for him, as if to make the patient relive precisely and vividly every step of her own pain. He then enumerates each helper spirit, called *nelegan*, in detail, and gives them special weapons and equipment: black beads, flame-coloured beads, tiger bones, armadillo bones and silver necklaces, but especially their pointed, penetrating hats.

At last the *nelegan* enter the patient's vagina, and after all this emotional preparation it is quite possible that she actually feels the penetration. The hats "light up" the route and this may also illuminate her own state of mind. Once inside, their itinerary moves across a landscape which is both the internal anatomy of a living body and an emotional geography of the psyche which inhabits it:

The nelegan set out, the nelegan march in a single file along Muu's road, as far as the Low Mountain,
The nelegan set out, the nelegan march in a single file along Muu's road, as far as the Short Mountain,
The nelegan set out, the nelegan march in a single file along Muu's road, as far as the Long Mountain,
The nelegan set out, the nelegan march in a single file along Muu's road, to Yala Pokuna Yala...

Line after line, the shaman enumerates the ridges and curves as they are passed by his helper spirits. The patient's pains take the form of an alligator and an octopus and Muu's own guards appear as a black tiger, a red animal or a dust-coloured animal. The *nelegan* tie down each of these in turn with an iron chain while it roars and slavers and tears at its surroundings with its claws and draws blood. We can only guess the effect of these descriptions upon the patient, but it must surely be profound. Finally, the *nelegan* reach the womb and use their hats as magical weapons to win a tournament with the spirits which they encounter there. Now begins the return journey. This must induce the birth by dilating the cervix and vaginal passage and the *nelegan* must draw the baby out behind them.

The shaman summons further reinforcements such as the armadillo, a Lord of the Burrowing Animals. Whereas on the inward journey the *nelegan* squeezed through in single file, on the return journey they come out marching four abreast.

In order for such a "cure" to work, the shaman takes a situation which exists on the emotional level, but with physical consequences, and which is essentially chaotic in its nature, and in what it might signify. The structure of the chant gives meaning to the patient's blockage and pain and gives them an elaborate and specific relationship to cosmic order. As with all shamanic journeys, it does

The story of the emergency expedition into a pregnant woman's womb, told in the primitive picture language of the Cuna people.

so in a narrative way which allows for the resolution of the problem through the convincing unfolding of events. This resolution induces a physiological process of release which we can see happening again and again in the most diverse healing situations throughout the world. It is the symbols themselves, existing primarily in the abstract realm of the mind or soul, which cause the desired changes in what may be called the physical world.

Documentary Reference

Sources and references

The Shamanic Worldview

Bibliographic references are given by
author, date of publication and (where
appropriate) page number. To save space,
articles by various authors collected in one
book are listed only once, under the name
of the book's editor. Thus, "Harner in
Doore 1988" refers to the article by Harner
incuded in the book edited by Doore and
will be listed under Doore. Where no other
source is given, information about India,
Sri Lanka and Siberia come from my own
fieldwork and translations from local
languages are my own.

What is a shaman?

I shall use the word "shamanism" as little
as the English language allows.
Communism, Feminism, Capitalism,
Buddhism – all these "-isms" are doctrines
or ideologies set up in relation to other
ideologies with texts, teachings and even
political aspirations. Shamans and their
communities have not generally done this,
and shamanic ideas and practices coexist
more or less freely with those of more
formalized systems. Perhaps the shaman's
activities should be called "shamanry", like
wizardry, and the shaman's professional
quality should be called "shamanship". At
the very least, since there is no unifying
ideology, we should talk of "shamanisms"
in the plural. I have concentrated on the

LEFT *A Gurung shaman from Nepal.*

shamanism of traditional societies because
these are the core of shamanic practice.
Some of the ideas and rites described may
be changed or no longer be practised today.
However, there is a current revival of
shamanism among some traditionally
shamanist peoples.

The most comprehensive worldwide survey is
Eliade 1964; see also Atkinson 1992; Peters and
Price-Williams, 1980. For examples worldwide,
Halifax 1979, Hoppál and von Sadowszky 1989.
"Shamanship" is from Atkinson 1989.
Shamanism different from possession, de Heusch
1981, disputed by Lewis 1989: 40ff. Frightened
little girls, Rasmussen quoted in Merkur 1991:
253–4.

Spirits and souls
Layers of the cosmos
Levels of reality
Concepts of power

The idea of a tree, pillar or mountain at the
centre of the world is found far beyond
shamanic cultures, as in the Mount Meru of
Buddhism or the pyramid-shaped ziggurats
of ancient Mesopotamia and Central
America. I have taken the bus past the Toda
land of the dead in the Nilgiri mountains of
south India. This place is called
euphemistically *am-nodr*, "That Land".

Spirits and souls: Multiple souls among North
American Indians, Hultkrantz, 1979 131; in
Amazonia, Harner 1972: 258ff and Luna 1984:
132. Wana soul and liver, Atkinson 1989: 110–11.
Eskimo names and souls, Nuttall 1992;
Lowenstein 1992: xxxiii, 93, 125; names and
species, Williamson quoted by Merkur 1991: 13–14.

Layers of the cosmos: Nganasan and Sakha/Yakut, Popov cited by Basilov 1984: 69. Sora sun victims, Vitebsky 1993. The Yagua artist's explanation of the Amazon cosmos is given (in French) in Chaumeil 1982: 49–53.

Levels of reality: Hmong shamans, Lemoine in Hoppál and Howard 1993: 111–19. Eskimo song, Lowenstein 1973: xxi. Inuit names, Nuttall 1992. Inuit soul, Gubser cited in Merkur 1991: 26–7. Christianization of Sora shamanists, Vitebsky 1995a. The terms "non-ordinary" or "separate" reality were made popular by Castaneda 1968 (and other titles).

Concepts of power: Sora transmission of spirit power, Vitebsky 1993: 53. Shamanism different from possession, de Heusch 1981. Women's subordination and powerlessness, Lewis 1989 – despite criticisms, this remains a classic analysis of the sociology of shamanism and possession. The word *payé*, Campbell 1989: 104–6. Dakota quotation, Fletcher quoted in Grim 1984: 5. Darts and phlegm in Amazonia, Luna 1986 and Luna and Amaringo 1991. Sakha/Yakut specialists, Platon Sleptsov personal communication and Gogolev 1992.

Regional Traditions

The religion of the stone age
Hunters, herders and farmers

In most hunting societies, women are not supposed to handle weapons or kill animals. Yet sexual taboos on the hunters show that women are involved symbolically in the men's activities. At the start of the spring whale hunt in Alaska, a woman lay down where the ice met the unfrozen sea with her body facing the village. Her husband's boat was turned as if returning from the hunt and the harpooner leaned over in silence and struck her body gently with the point of his harpoon. Then the woman walked home without looking back. For the rest of the hunt, she did not move but sat on the sleeping bench, because every domestic action would affect her husband's hunt adversely. If she scrubbed the floor, the whale's skin would be too thin; if she used a knife, his harpoon line would break.

The religion of the stone age: Lommel 1966, reviewed by various writers in *Current Anthropology* 1970: 39–48. Rock art of North America and Africa: Lewis-Williams and Dowson 1988. Rock art from the former Soviet Union: illustrated summary in English, Hoppál in Siikala and Hoppál: 132–49. The "Ice Man", *National Geographic* Oct 1988: 36–67. Trois Frères cave, Campbell 1959: 306–11; palaeolithic shamans, pp.229–312.

Hunters, herders and farmers: The term "master of spirits" for the shaman probably comes originally from Shirokogoroff's extraordinary, idiosyncratic and rare book *The Psychomental Complex of the Tungus* (1935). Hunting and planting, Campbell 1959: 66; 229ff. "Worship and brutality", Lowenstein, 1993: xxxiv. Master or Mistress of the Animals, Siikala 1978: 63; Reichel-Dolmatoff 1971; Hamayon 1990 (in French). Desana seduction of animals, Reichel-Dolmatoff 1971: 220–21. Siberian shaman's dance, Hamayon in Thomas and Humphrey 1994: 61. Korean shamans, Kendall, personal communication. Female shamans, Tsing 1993; Vitebsky 1993; Kendall 1985, 1988. The above account of the Eskimo hunter's wife refers to the turn of the century and was collected recently from living memory, Lowenstein 1992: 47.

Siberia and Mongolia
South and East Asia
North America

Shamanism in Siberia is largely a thing of the past. The classic literature on this region is vast. Most is in Russian and very little of this has ever been translated into any western language. Some of the Siberian material presented here has been translated for the first time.

Siberia and Mongolia: The best overview of Siberia in English is Siikala 1978 (see also Eliade 1964). Other excellent overviews are Basilov 1984 (in Russian, partly translated in Balzer 1990) and Hamayon 1990 (in French). Books edited by Diószegi, Hoppál and their colleagues contain numerous short articles and Diószegi (1968) is an enjoyable read. Some important longer works are translated in Balzer 1990 and Michael 1963, which includes Anisimov's material on the Evenk clan. Extracts from various translations are reprinted in Halifax 1979. Journeying shaman distinct from clan shaman, Humphrey in Thomas and Humphrey 1994: 199–200. For Mongolia, there is less in English: the standard work is Heissig 1980; see also Humphrey 1980. Shamans and Genghis Khan, Humphrey in Thomas and Humphrey 1994: 201ff; see also Vitebsky 1974.

South and East Asia: India: Vitebsky 1993. Nepal: Peters 1981 and article in Nicholson 1987; Desjarlais 1989; Sagant in Hamayon 1982; Mumford 1989. Southeast Asia: Wana, Atkinson 1989; Iban, Graham 1987; Malay peninsula, Chewong, Howell 1989; Batek, Endicott 1979; Temiar, Roseman 1991; Hmong, Lemoine in Doore 1988: 63–72; Meratus Dayak, Tsing 1993. China and Japan: Blacker 1986; Anagnost 1987; various authors in Hoppál and Howard 1993 and in *Shaman*: 1(1) 1993. Korea: Kendall 1985; 1988; 1993; Kim 1989. Buddhism: in Sri Lanka, Kapferer 1983; in Nepal, Mumford 1989.

North America: Northwest coast, Eliade 1964: 309; Salish: Jilek 1982; Harner 1982: 70–71, 92; Hultkrantz 1992: 61–70. Lame Deer, Lame Deer and Erdoes 1972: 136–7; shaman different from medicine-person, Hultkrantz 1979: 86–90; Washo, Handelman 1967; Ojibway, Grim 1986. Classic anthropology: numerous works by Franz Boas, eg discussed in Lévi-Strauss 1963: 175–8; Paul Radin, eg 1920, 1945; further references in *Handbook of North American Indians* (Sturtevant 1978). Excerpts in Halifax 1979. Eskimo/Inuit: Lowenstein 1992, 1993; Kleivan and Sonne 1985; Merkur 1985, 1991; Rasmussen 1929; Saladin d'Anglure in Hoppál and Pentikainen 1993: 146–50 and in Hoppál and Howard 1993: 160–8.

South and Central America
The rest of the world
His ears are his ornaments,
His ears are his ornaments,
They are the white feathers of the harpy eagle.

A Yakut shaman being dismembered, painted by the artist, Timofei Stepanof.

When he is thus adorned, he is fierce;
Then he is armed with his bow;
Thus he is adorned.

Now they take his bow away from him,
They take it away.
Thus they take away his ornaments,
Taking it away, they put it on the platform of the sun.
(Desana spell for warding off a were-jaguar)

South and Central America: sources include especially Langdon and Baer 1992; *The Handbook of South American Indians* (Steward 1963). Chants: Luna 1986; Luna and Amaringo 1991; Luna in Langdon and Baer 1992. Desana: Reichel-Dolmatoff, 1971, 1978, especially 1975: 118 (turning into jaguars), 128 (spell against were-jaguars), 46 (hollow jaguar bone). *Vegetalista* spell, Luna 1986: 243. History of violence, Taussig 1987. Central America: Huichol, Myerhoff 1974; Furst 1976: 120–33; Mazatec, Wasson et al 1974; Furst 1976: 75–88; Munn in Harner 1973: 86–122. Cuna/Kuna, Holmer and Wassén 1947; Lévi-Strauss 1963: 186–205.

The rest of the world: Eliade 1964. Australia and New Guinea: Elkin 1977; Descola and Lory in Hamayon 1982; Herdt and Stephen 1989: 103–4. Africa: Katz 1982; giraffe quotation adapted from Biesele, quoted in Halifax 1979: 54–62. Idea of flight widespread in Africa, Lewis 1986 : chapter 5. Europe: ancient Greece, Dodds 1951; Celts, Matthews 1991; Saami, Hungary and Northern Europe, various papers in Hoppál and Pentikainen 1992; Hoppál 1994; Siikala and Hoppál 1992.

Becoming a Shaman

Who becomes a shaman?
Initiation and instruction

Dyukhade's experience is typically Siberian. As it unfolds, we see that it is not only animal species which have a "Master", but also various states of mind and forms of human experience. The Nanai story comes from Shternberg, who believed that sexuality was at the root of the shaman's experience.

Who becomes a shaman?: The initiatory illness is described in many sources, some cited by Eliade 1964. Siberian shaman's drum, Basilov 1984: 121–2. Henry's power dream, Handelman 1967: 447–8; and his payment of the older shaman, p.450. Dreams and marriage of the future Sora shaman, Vitebsky 1993: 19–21, 56–61. Shamanic power purchased among the Jivaro, Harner 1972. Uncontrolled Evenk spirit, Shirokogoroff in Basilov 1984: 143. Nanai (Gol'd) shaman, Shternberg 1936: 354–5 (my translation). Dyukhade's story, Popov 1936: 84ff, discussed in Basilov 1984: 59–63. A similar Siberian initiatory story from Popov is translated in Diószegi 1968: 137–45, reprinted in Halifax 1979: 37–49. Allergy to turtle: Langdon and Baer 1992: 105–6.

Initiation and instruction: Uvavnuk's story, Rasmussen 1929: 122–3. Korean teacher's remark, Kendall 1993: 22. Siberian iron cradle, Popov 1947: 286–9. Alaskan shaman inside the womb/igloo, Lowenstein 1993: 43–4; bound with an "umbilical cord", Lowenstein, 1992: 151. For Inuit initiation, see also Merkur 1985. Winnebago boy's failed vision quest, Radin 1920. Dyukhade's dismemberment, see previous section.

Trance and ecstasy

"What tells me that Dau isn't fully learned", says a Kung Bushman, " is the way he behaves ... His eyes are rolling all over the place. If your eyes are rolling, you can't stare at sickness. You have to be absolutely steady to see sickness, steady-eyed, no shivering and shaking."

Trance different from ecstasy, Rouget 1987. Siberian shamans' journeys, Basilov 1984: 152. Kung Bushman quotation above, Katz 1982: 105. Trance and possession, Bourguignon 1976, Peters and Price-Williams 1980.

Helpers and teachers
Voyages to other realms
Battles with hostile spirits

In Siberia, the Oroch thought that shamans could fly to the sun, but that this was pretty pointless except for the sake of the exploit itself. This journey is extremely dangerous because of a girl who lives on the sun. Just looking at her face can blind you and going near her could burn you up. The path to the sun passes via the moon. The shaman's soul would begin its dizzying journey on a winged horse, then it would rush along on a roll of thread and on a rag ball with wings, fly between the constellations, then change on to a bird and finally approach the sun in a winged iron boat. On the return journey he would descend to earth in a winged iron coffin. Nanai shamans used to visit the sun on serious business, in quest of children's souls for infertile women.

Helpers and teachers: Sora spirit helpers, Vitebsky 1993. *Vegetalistas*: instruction of apprentice, Luna 1986: 51; foreign and extraterrestrial doctors, pp.94–5; plants as teachers, pp.62, 54–5; ant of knowledge, p.49; see also Luna and Amaringo 1991 throughout. Henry's mishandling of the weather, Handelman 1967: 448–9. Homer's *Odyssey* translated by Edward Fitzgerald; many other translations are available.

Voyages to other realms: Sora shaman's journey, Vitebsky 1993; 18–9; Siberian shaman's journeys: Avrorin and Kosminsky; Smoliak, both cited in Basilov 1984: 67–8. Salish canoe journey, Jilek 1982; Harner 1982: 70–71, 92; Hultkrantz 1992: 61–70. Wana spirit boat, Atkinson 1989: 159ff. Nepalese shaman's journey on this earth, Desjarlais 1989. The adventures of Odysseus are told in Homer's *Odyssey*, available in many translations. *The Phantom Tollbooth* is by Norton Juster. The moon as land of the dead in Nepal: Sagant 1982. John Glenn and the Russian wise man on the moon: my fieldwork. Near-death experiences, Ring 1984.

Battles with hostile spirits: Nepalese shaman's remark: personal communication from Judith Pettigrew. Nenets, Oroch and Nanai ideas about sun and moon, Basilov 1984: 67. Altai shaman's journey to underworld, Potanin cited in Eliade 1964:201ff . Warao shaman, Wilbert in Furst 1972: 64. Sora war party's song, Vitebsky 1993: 122ff. Dolgan shaman, Popov cited by Basilov, translated in Balzer 1990: 180–81. Smallpox among the Even, Alekseyev 1994; many similar battles in Ksenofontov 1930.

Music, dance and words

And in the vast jungle filling with night terrors there arose the Word. A word that was more than word ... this was something far beyond language and yet still far from song. Something that had not yet discovered vocalization but was more than word ... blinding me with the realization that I had just witnessed the birth of music. (Alejo Carpentier on the song of a shaman in the Venezuelan forest, *The Lost Steps*, New York: Knopf 1974)

How shamans make things happen with words, Vitebsky 1993; Lévi-Strauss 1963: 187–205. Altai shaman, Potanin in Eliade 1964: 201. Organizing ambiguous impressions, Walsh 1990: 118–9. Icaro song, Luna and Amaringo 1991: 39–40; plant spirits, Luna 1986: 97–102. Drum in Siberia, Dolgikh in Diószegi and Hoppál 1978: 341–51; Vajnstejn in Diószegi 1968: 331–8. Siberian dance, Zhornitskaya in Diószegi and Hoppál 1978: 299–307. Korean dance, Kendall 1985: 10–11. Desana incest warning, Reichel-Dolmatoff 1971: 166ff. Important general discussions of drumming, Rouget 1985; Achterberg 1985: 41–5; Jilek 1982. Drumming experiment by Neher 1962, criticized by Rouget 1985: 172–6 and Achterberg 1985: 43–4. Drumming pulse rates, Walsh 1990: 176; Achterberg 1985: 43–5. Dyukhade catching his drum on the wing, Popov 1947: 86–7. Gurung girls, Alan Macfarlane and Judith Pettigrew, personal communication. Music as organizing and socializing trance, Rouget 1985. For melody, see also Roseman 1991.

Costumes and equipment
Shamanic botany: hallucinogens
Blacksmiths! Blacksmiths!
How many blacksmiths have I
Who forge men!
What have you forged for me? Antlers for my back.
How many bellows? How many forgers of metal parts?
Metal, metal, metal
Iron filings
I am gathering
Making them much sharper
Metal, metal, metal.

Costumes and equipment: Siberian shaman's costume, Graceva in Diószegi and Hoppál 1978: 315–23; Djakonova in Diószegi and Hoppál 1978: 325–39; Prokofyeva in Michael 1963: 124–56. Crystals, Harner 1980: 109–112; Ripinsky-Naxon 1993: 123–6. Korean shaman's equipment, Kendall 1993. Blacksmith in Siberia, Eliade 1964: 470–2; song quoted adapted from Vasilevich, in Diószegi 1968: 369–70. Asatchaq and his *kikituk*, Lowenstein 1992: 148–9.

Shamanic botany: Important works on hallucinogenic plants include Harner 1973; Furst 1972; Furst 1976; Schultes and Hoffman 1979; Schultes 1990. These are mostly concerned with South and Central America. *Amanita muscaria* mushroom in Asia, Wasson in Furst 1972: 185–200; Furst 1976: 89–95, 96ff. Plants as spirit teachers, Luna, 1986: 115; spirits of trees quoted,

101–2. Master of the *Viho* plant, Reichel-Dolmatoff 1971. Drug-taking as male initiation, Schultes and Hofmann 1979: 166; Langdon and Baer. Huichol quotation, Furst 1972; xiii. Sharing of drugs or visions between healer and patient, La Barre in Furst 1972: 275; Schultes and Hofmann 1973: 163. Patient's review of own life, Luna 1986: 161–2. *Ayahuasca* incident, Luna 1986: 154–5. Eliade on degeneration, 1964: 401. Fatigue or stress, Furst 1972: ix. La Barre on gods, in Furst 1972: 268. Mushrooms' deadly verdict, Wasson *et al.* 1974: blood or saliva of Christ, pp.xiv–xv; direct quotations taken from pp.33, 71, 79, 93. This book is rare but part of the text is reprinted in Halifax 1979: 195–213.

Tricks of the trade
The shaman's multiple nature
A shaman's effect is often achieved by magically creating a resemblance between an object and the person who is to be affected. A Wana shaman sharpens a piece of bamboo, aims it at a victim and sings:

You, oh spirit of bamboo,
make light as I throw.
Over there is the heart to head for.
Make the liver fall out.

Tricks of the trade: Wana spell, Atkinson 1989: 72. Marco Polo: *The Travels*, Penguin edition, p.110. Henry's remark, Handelman 1967: 457. Story of the Nepalese shaman's escape told to me by his grandson. Alaskan *tupitkaq* (in Greenland dialect *tupilak*), Lowenstein 1993: 42–3. Quesalid's story from Boas, discussed by Lévi-Strauss 1963: 175–8. Siberian shaman's séance, Shatilov quoted in Basilov 1984: 123–4.

The imagery of death (and rebirth) is a common theme in much shamanic equipment.

The shaman's multiple nature: Shamans and jaguars, Reichel-Dolmatoff 1975: 43, 108; see also chapter 2, above. Batek and Chewong respectively, Endicott 1979: 139–41; Howell 1989: 103. On ethnic violence in South America, Taussig 1987. Sora shaman's monkey song, Vitebsky 1993: 18–19. Henry's Hindu spirit, Handelman 1967: 451–2. "Owners" of body parts in Mongolia and Siberia, Siikala in Siikala and Hoppál 1992: 62, and compare a similar idea among the Cuna of Panama on pp.158–9 of the present book. Transvestism: general, Halifax 1979: 22–7; Siberia, Shternberg in Dunn and Dunn 1974: 77; Basilov in Diószegi and Hoppál 1978: 281; Alaska, Lowenstein 1992: 140; North America, Williams 1986: 19, 35–6 and for gay movement, chapter 10.

Death of the shaman

An old shaman in Nepal had been training his son for years, but withheld the most important and powerful secrets until the last days of his life. On his deathbed, he gave these to his son, saying, "You were young and impulsive, I was afraid you would misuse them. But when I am gone you will be the senior shaman, you will have to use these powers responsibly." Yet even now the younger man cannot be sure whether he has received the full richness of his father's knowledge, or whether he will have to build this up himself from experience and practice.

Darkhat Mongols, Badamkhatan 1986: 187–8; Sakha, Ksenofontov 1992: 59–60; Nepal, Judith Pettigrew, personal communication. See also Kenin-Lopsan in Diószegi and Hoppál 1978: 291–8.

Shamans and Clients

Healing the sick, rescuing lost souls
Divining
Obtaining animals

Difficult times,
shortages of meat
have smitten everyone;
stomachs hollow,
meat-trays empty,
Aj-ja-japapé.

Can you see out there?

The men are coming home,
dragging seals
towards our village!
Aj-ja-japapé.

Joy has distorted
everything in sight:
the leather boats lift themselves
away from their ropes,
the straps follow them,
the earth itself
floats freely in the air!
Aj-ja-japapé.
(Lowenstein 1973)

Healing the sick: Wana patient rescued by flattery, Atkinson 1989: 166. Fisherman's seduction, Luna 1986: 80–82; Virote darts: 112–4. Siberia: Pole Star, Bogoraz-Tan 1939: 41. Rescue of Sakha/Yakut woman, Ksenofontov 1930: 179–83, discussed in Campbell 1959: 258–63 and in Ducey 1979. Monkey incubus, Freeman 1967. Health in Siberia, Alekseyev 1994.

Divining: Paviotso shaman, Park cited in Eliade 1964: 303–4. Sakha/Yakut shaman's dreams, Shternberg 1936: 224–6. Dyukhade's interrogation of the landscape, Popov cited by Basilov, translated in Balzer 1990: 20. Asatchaq's flight, Lowenstein 1993: 140–44.

Obtaining animals: Batek, Endicott 1972:20. Eskimo who became a whale, Lowenstein 1993: 90–94; Asatchaq's visit to the moon and women's pots, pp.19–20, 150. Hunting more basic than healing, also Siberian fertility dances, Hamayon in Hoppál and Pentikainen 1992: 134–5. Vai-Mahse's cave, Reichel-Dolmatoff 1971: 82–3, 130–1. Dyukhade, Popov 1936.

Protecting the community
Shamans and the state
Dramas and roles

There can be sudden twists in the status accorded to shamans. During the 1970s in South Korea, shamanism was marginalized. The elite regarded it as primitive in comparison to the more civilized Confucianism and shamanism was discouraged officially as a matter of state policy. However political circumstances in the 1980s led to the official encouragement of shamanism as an authentic expression of the "Korean people".

Protecting the community: Shaman in community, Vitebsky 1993; Atkinson 1989. Evenk clan river, Anisimov in Michael 1963. Names among Eskimo, Nuttall 1992; among Sora, Vitebsky 1993. Warfare among Achuar and Baruya, Descola and Lory 1982 (in French). For New Guinea, see also Herdt and Stephen 1989. Sorcery among Sora, Vitebsky 1993: 103–9, 115–18; among Washo, Handelman 1967. *Vegetalista* and mermaid, Luna 1986: 80–2. Asatchaq's duel, Lowenstein 1992: 145–8. Shaman's-eye view, Anisimov in Michael 1963: 106. Sora rice-flour effigy, Vitebsky 1993: 227–8.

Shamans and the state: Best discussion is Thomas and Humphrey 1994. Manchu empire: Humphrey's paper in this book. Genghis Khan, Humphrey 1980; Vitebsky 1974. Achuar and Baruya, see previous section. Bureaucratic helper spirits, Vitebsky 1993: 56–61. Ghost Dance, La Barre 1970. Women's protest, Lewis 1989, questioned by Kendall 1985: 24–5. Korean celestial kings, Kendall, 1993: 20. War and violence, Kim 1989; Taussig 1987.

Dramas and roles: Emotion and drama at shamanic séance, Atkinson 1989: 230–52; Vitebsky 1993; Sora woman who dies to save her baby, Vitebsky 1993: 173–5, 180–7; step-by-step detection, pp.99–120. Theatre and performance theory, Kendall 1993, 1995. Hidden script versus constant formation, Kapferer 1983: 9. Eliade quotation, 1964: 8. Stabbing the air, Kendall 1988: 7. Sakha/Yakut dance, Zhornitskaya in Diószegi and Hoppál 1978: 299–307.

A summary of shamanic procedure.
Uvavnuk, the Inuit woman who became a powerful shaman after being struck by a meteor, afterward repeated the following song incessantly:

The great sea
Has set me adrift,
It moves me as a weed in a great river,
Earth and the great weather
Move me,
Have carried me away
And move my inward parts with joy

Her sense of intoxication spread to everyone else in the house and without prompting they all began to confess their own misdeeds and to accuse each other. And those accused also confessed and lifted up their arms as if to fling away all evil, which was was blown away like a speck of dust with the words, "Away with it, away with it!" Shortly before she died, Uvavnuk announced that she would protect her people from hunger. She obtained a large number of whales, seals and walrus from the Mistress of the Animals. The next year, they had a greater abundance of game than at any other time within living memory.

Summary of procedure: Inuit references, Rasmussen 1929: 123–9. The diagram is my own.

Understanding shamans

Early impressions
Shamanism in the history of religion
Communist regimes
Are shamans mentally ill?
Do shamans really heal?

A shaman and client are often more closely bound together psychically than a doctor and patient. The view of the shaman as a "wounded healer", based on Jungian ideas of the analyst, combines images of the shaman's own vulnerability and of his or her power. This is not a contradiction, since the power is based on the vulnerability. In the typical medical model, the doctor is presented largely as invulnerable and all-capable, while the patient remains passive and helpless. In the Jungian model, both

A shaman flies to the other realm with the help of his animal spirits.

the analyst and the patient have both wounds and healing powers. The analyst projects her own experience of being wounded onto the patient in order to know the patient emotionally; while the patient may initially be unaware of his self-healing abilities and project them onto the analyst but will later become able to take them back. This view seems close to much shamanic healing. For example, Sora dialogues show sick people taking an active part in their own healing.

Early impressions: The Devil in South America, Reichel-Dolmatoff 1975: 3–4; Oviedo quotation: 8–9. Shamans in Siberia, Hoppál in Siikala and Hoppál 1992: 176–81. Medieval Mongolia quotation, Vitebsky 1974: 36. For 18th-century Europe, see Flaherty 1992.

Other religions: Shamans and origin of religion, La Barre 1970 and in Furst 1972. Pure versus degraded religion, Eliade 1964: 401; his quotation on history of religion, xvii. Manchu Shaman Book, Stary reviewed by Kolhami in *Shaman*: 1(1), 1993: 63. Phenomenology and theology, Grim 1984: 26–7. Kublai's reincarnation, Vitebsky 1974: 39 n.5; Samsonov's dolls, Humphrey 1980: 251. Sri Lankan exorcism, Kapferer 1983: 270–1.

Communist regimes: Soviet Union, Humphrey 1983: 402–17; Balzer in *Shaman* 1(2) 1993; Vitebsky 1992: 228, 239ff; China, Anagnost 1987; Shi Kun in *Shaman* 1(1), 1993: 48–57.

Mental illness/healing: Jungian parallel above: Samuels *et al* 1986: 65. Shaman and psychoanalyst, Lévi-Strauss 1963: 198–204; Vitebsky 1993: 236–59. Shaman as insane, Basilov 1984: 139; Devereux 1961. Shaman as sane, Handelman 1967; Noll 1983. Discussion in Lewis 1989: 160–84. Shaman not schizophrenic, Noll 1983 and in Nicholson 1987: 54–6; Walsh 1990: 224–6; Silverman 1967. Freudian analysis of Sakha/Yakut shaman, Ducey 1979. Little girl dialogue, Vitebsky 1993: 3–4, 171–2.

Kinds of consciousness

"Then I didn't really fly, Don Juan. I flew in my imagination, in my mind alone ... If I had tied myself to a rock with a heavy chain, I would have flown just the same, because my body had nothing to do with my flying." Don Juan looked at me incredulously. "If you tie yourself to a rock," he said, "I'm afraid you will have to

fly holding the rock with its heavy chain." (Castaneda: *The teachings of Don Juan*) Second paragraph, references in Walsh 1990: Part V; see also Atkinson 1992: 310. Consciousness the same among shamans, Buddhists, etc., Doore 1988: 223, disputed by Walsh 1990: 215–6. Alternative view in Walsh 1990: chapters 17, 18. The "Mapping of Nonordinary Reality Project" is Harner's. Zen awareness, Suzuki 1970: 128. Chini's struggle, Kendall 1995. Endorphins, special issue of *Ethos* 1982.

New shamanic movements
The cosmos within

An elderly shaman among the Inuit, who could no longer move about physically, gave a symbolic acknowledgement to this physical disability by making the interior of the igloo serve as a map of the cosmos. The raised platform became the land, the floor was the sea, while the spiral arrangement of the igloo's snow-blocks became the heavens with the ice-window serving as the sun and the door-opening as the moon. The shaman transposed the different parts of the igloo throughout the universe and so could travel there when he needed to locate game for his community.

New shamanic movements: Good books, with diverse viewpoints on the current upsurge of interest in shamanism, include Walsh 1990; Doore 1988; Harner 1982; Larsen 1976; Goodman 1990; Achterberg 1987; Kalweit 1984; Nicholson 1987; Ripinsky-Naxon 1993. Don Juan books, Castaneda 1968 and others. Harner: "core shamanism", 1982; "shamanic counselling", his article in Doore 1988; the quotation given is from a publicity leaflet. Song of the air, Kelly 1993: 28. Interview with *The Shamen* pop group from French magazine *Actuel* for Jan–Feb 1993: 64–5. For problems with publicity for native shamans, Joralemon 1990.

The cosmos within: Inuit shaman in igloo, above, Saladin d'Anglure in Hoppál and Pentikainen 1993: 147. Leopards or psychosis, Vitebsky 1993: 245. Flight of Nepalese shaman, Desjarlais 1989; quotations, p.303. White man's and Indian medicine, Achterberg in Doore 1988: 119. Expedition into the womb, Holmer and Wassén 1947, discussed by Lévi-Strauss 1963: 186–205; limitations to patient's understanding of the words, Sherzer 1983: 134.

Directory of Peoples

This glossary lists only peoples who are referred to often in this book and who are likely to be unfamiliar to many readers. Especially for smaller peoples without a state of their own, ethnic names are unstable and are often likely to be the names of clans, subgroups or places where they live now or where they came from in the past. In addition, many peoples are known to outsiders by names which they themselves find insulting. I have used their own names wherever possible, although this sometimes causes problems. For example, there is now no fully acceptable word to cover all the groups previously known as "Eskimo".

Buryat A people speaking a language close to Mongolian and living around Lake Baikal in Siberia.

Bushman See Kung.

Chukchi A small group in the far northeast of Siberia, facing Alaska across the Bering Strait.

Cuna, Kuna A people of Panama.

Desana A group in the upper Amazon, partially overlapping with the Tukano.

Eskimo A people or group of peoples spread around the arctic coastline in North America, Greenland and Siberia. The name "Eskimo", meaning "Eaters of raw flesh", was given them by neighbouring North American "Indians" and is now out of favour. But although every group has its own name for itself, these are very little known worldwide, except for the Inuit in Canada. Moreover, there is no other collective word for all such groups, so that I have been obliged to retain this word more than I should have liked.

Evén, Evenk Two groups of Siberian hunters and reindeer herders, previously generally known by the name Tungus. The word "shaman" comes from the Evenk language.

Gurung A non-Aryan people in western Nepal, probably of Central Asian origin.

Huichol A native people of Mexico, widely known for their use of the *peyote* cactus.

Inuit The main Canadian branch of the "Eskimo". The name means "humans".

Kung A people of the Kalahari Desert on the border of Botswana and Namibia, called Bushmen by outsiders (see San).

Kwakiutl A native people of British Columbia, Canada.

Lapp An outsiders' name for Saami.

Manchu A people of Manchuria, in northeast China. Linguistically related to the Tungus forest tribes, they became the modern emperors of China.

Matses A group in northern Peru. Noted for elaborately decorating their bodies to look like jaguars.

Matsigenka Neighbours of the Matses in Peru, but sharing little in the way of traditions.

Mazatec A native people of Mexico, who make an extensive use of *psilocybe* mushrooms.

Mestizo Not really an ethnic name: in Latin America, populations of mixed Indian and European blood. In parts of the upper Amazon, their plant-inspired shaman is called a *vegetalista*.

Mongol The main inhabitants of Mongolia, rulers in the Middle Ages of a great empire of their own; their rulers also became the emperors of China.

Nganasan A small group of hunters and reindeer herders in northwest Siberia.

Saami A people of northern Scandinavia, known by outsiders as Lapp.

Sakhá Called Yakut by Russian colonists of Siberia. Sakhá was reinstated as their official name in 1990.

Salish A coastal people on the border of Washington State, USA and British Columbia, Canada.

San A people of the Kalahari desert, called Bushmen by outsiders (see Kung).

Sora An indigenous "tribal" people in the state of Orissa, India, speaking a Mundu language.

Tungus see Evén, Evenk

vegetalista see Mestizo

Wana A small group on the island of Sulawesi in Indonesia.

Washo A people of the California-Nevada border.

Yakut The common Russian name for the Sakhá of Siberia.

New Shamanic Movements

Is shamanship a universal human potential? Could I become a shaman? Increasing numbers of people in modern society are asking these questions. The number of organizations, magazines and workshops concerned with shamanism, or claiming to be, is now very large. Not all of these are of equal authenticity or integrity, and since shamanic practice can be spiritually and psychologically highly provoking readers are advised to examine them very searchingly before making any substantial personal commitment. Some of the more significant addresses are listed here, but the inclusion or omission of any organization from this list does not necessarily imply any endorsement or criticism.

Many forms of neo-shamanism use elements from North American native religions which I have characterized in this book as not strictly shamanic. In addition, particularly in North America, native organizations have started to criticize some of these systems for cultural imperialism or intellectual piracy. There are numerous native organisations which combine in various ways the teaching of outsiders with a lobby for their own cultural regeneration. It is not possible to list these here. While some would not welcome wide publicity, others advertize in the main magazines.

Shamanic Film and Video Archive
PO Box 691,
Bearsville, NY 12409, USA,
phone/fax (914) 679 9761
Gathers information on all existing film and video showing shamanic activity and collects copies wherever possible. Publishes *The Journey Journal.*

Foundation for Shamanic Studies
PO Box 1939, Mill Valley, CA 94942, USA
phone (415) 380 8282
Founded by Michael Harner, an anthropologist who has worked mainly in the upper Amazon and a pioneer in developing a form of shamanic practice based partly on authentic elements from traditional cultures. Publishes the journal *Shamanism* and runs courses, mainly in North America.

Cross Cultural Shamanism Network
PO Box 430, Willits, CA 95490, USA
phone (707) 459 0486
Publishes *Shaman's Drum: A Journal of Experiential Shamanism*, containing articles, news, advertisements, book reviews.

Scandinavian Centre for Shamanic Studies
Artillerivej 63/140,
DK 2300 Copenhagen S
Denmark
phone (+45) 31 54 28 08
(Run by Jonathan Horwitz; Representative in UK: Shamanic Workshops in Britain, 61 Eldon Road, London N22 5ED, England, phone 0181 888 8178)
Offers courses in Scandinavia, Britain and other European countries in English and Danish.

Sacred Hoop
28 Cowl Street, Evesham, Worcs WR11 4PL, UK,
phone (01386) 446 552
For events and advertisers based in UK.

Circle of the Sacred Earth
21 Aaron Street, Melrose, MA 02176,
phone (617) 665 6032
Workshops in shamanic spirituality

International Society for Shamanic Research
PO Box 1195, Szeged, H-6701 Hungary
Associated with Mihály Hoppál and colleagues (see bibliography). Organizes conferences and publication of (mainly anthropological) research. Publishes *Shaman: an International Journal for Shamanistic Research*

Bibliography

This bibliography contains sources quoted and is also a guide to further reading. In a vast literature, it is inevitably highly selective and there are many hundreds of titles which I should have liked to include. I have given only works in English except where I have used works in other languages as sources.

For many titles, paperbacks, reprints and other editions may be available and it has not been possible to list these here. To save space, articles mentioned in the notes but published in a collective book are not listed separately here, but the books are listed under the editor's name.

Achterberg, J. *Imagery in Healing: Shamanism and Modern Medicine* Shambala, Boston, 1987

Alekseyev, A.A. "Healing Techniques among Evén Shamans" translated by S. Muravyev and P. Vitebsky in *The Journey Journal* 2(2): 1–3, 1984

Anagnost, A.S. "Politics and Magic in Contemporary China" in *Modern China* 13(1): 40–61, 1987

Atkinson, J.M. *The Art and Politics of Wana Shamanship* University of California Press, Berkeley, 1989

Atkinson, J.M. "Shamanisms Today" in *Annual Review of Anthropology* 21: 307–30, 1992

Badamkhatan, S. "Les Chamanistes du Bouddha vivant", translated from Mongol by M.D. Even in *Etudes Mongoles et Sibériennes* 71–207, 1986

Balzer, M.M. *Shamanism: Soviet Studies of Traditional Religion in Siberia and Central Asia* M.E. Sharpe, Armonk, New York, 1990

Basilov, V.N. *Izbranniki Dukhov [Chosen by the Spirits]* Politizdat, Moscow, 1984

Bogoraz-Tan, V.G. *Chukchi [The Chukchi]* part II, Leningrad, 1939

Bourguignon, E. *Possession* Chandler and Sharp, San Francisco, 1976

Campbell, A.T. *To Square with Genesis: Causal Statements and Shamanic Ideas in Wayapi* Edinburgh University Press, Edinburgh, 1989

Campbell, Joseph *The Masks of God: Primitive Mythology* Viking Penguin, New York, 1959

Castaneda, C. *The Teachings of Don Juan: a Yaqui Way of Knowledge* University of California Press, Berkeley, 1968

Chaumeil, J.-P. "Représentation du monde d'un Chamane Yagua [A Yagua Shaman's Representation of the World]" in Hamayon, 1982

de Heusch, L. "Possession and Shamanism" in his *Why Marry Her? Society and Symbolic Structures* Cambridge University Press, Cambridge, 1981

Desjarlais, R.R. "Healing through Images: the Magical Flight and Healing Geography of Nepali Shamans" in *Ethos* 17(3): 289–307, 1989

Devereux, G. "Shamans as Neurotics" in *American Anthropologist* 63(5): 1088–93, 1961

Dioszégi, V. *Tracing Shamans in Siberia: the Story of an Ethnographical Research Expedition* Humanities Press, New York, 1968a

Dioszégi, V. (ed) *Popular Beliefs and Folklore Tradition in Siberia* Indiana University, Boomington, 1968b

Dioszégi, V. and M. Hoppál (eds) *Shamanism in Siberia* Akadémiai Kiadó, Budapest, 1978

Dodds, E.R. *The Greeks and the Irrational* University of California, Berkeley and Los Angeles, 1951

Doore, G. *Shaman's Path: Healing, Personal Growth, and Empowerment* Shambala, Boston, 1988

Ducey, C. "The Shaman's Dream Journey: Psychoanalytic and Structural Complementarity in Myth Interpretation" in *The Psychoanalytic Study of Society* 8: 71–117, 1979

Edsman, C.M. (ed) *Studies in Shamanism* Almqvist and Wiksell, Stockholm, 1967

Eliade, M. *Shamanism: Archaic Techniques of Ecstasy* Pantheon, New York, 1964

Elkin, A.P. *Aboriginal Men of High Degree* St Martin's Press, New York, 1977

Endicott *Batek Negrito religion* Clarendon Press, Oxford, 1979

Ethos "Special Issue on Shamans and Endorphins" 10(4), 1982

Flaherty, G. *Shamanism and the Eighteenth Century* Princeton University Press, Princeton, 1992

Freeman, D. "Shaman and Incubus" in *The Psychoanalytic Study of Society* 4: 315–44, 1964

Furst, P.T. (ed) *Flesh of the Gods: the Ritual Use of Hallucinogens* Praeger, New York, 1972

Furst, P.T. *Hallucinogens and Culture* Chandler and Sharp, San Francisco, 1976

Gogolev, A.I. "Dualism in the Traditional Belief of the Yakuts" in *Anthropology and Archaeology of Eurasia* 31(2): 70–84, 1992

Goodman, F.D. *Where the Spirits Ride the Wind: Trance Journey and Other Ecstatic Experiences* Indiana University Press, Boomington, 1990

Graham, P. *Iban Shamanism: an Analysis of the Ethnographic Literature* Australian National University, Canberra, 1987

Grim, J. *The Shaman: Patterns of Siberian and Ojibway Healing* University of Oklahoma Press, Norman, 1984

Halifax, J. *Shamanic Voices: a Survey of Visionary Narratives* Dutton, New York, 1979

Hamayon, R. *La Chasse à l'âme: esquisse d'une théorie du Chamanisme Sibérien [Hunting the Soul: Outline of a Theory of Siberian Shamanism]* Société d'ethnologie, Nanterre, 1990

Hamayon, R. (ed) "Voyages Chamaniques [Shamanic Journeys] II" in *L'Ethnographie 78* (special issue), 1982

Hamayon, R. (ed) "Special Issue on Shamanism" in *Diogenes* 158, 1992

Handelman, D. "The Development of a Washo Shaman" in *Ethnology* 6(4): 444–64, 1967

Harner, M. *The Jivaro: People of the Sacred Waterfalls* Doubleday, Garden City, 1972

Harner, M. *The Way of the Shaman* Bantam, New York, 1982

Harner, M. (ed) *Hallucinogens and Shamanism* Oxford University Press, Oxford, 1973

Heissig, W. *The Religions of Mongolia* Routledge, London, 1980

Herdt, G.H. and M. Stephen *The Religious Imagination in New Guinea* Rutgers University Press, New Brunswick, 1989

Holmer, N.M. and H. Wassén *Mu-Iglala or the Way of Muu: a Medicine Song from the Cunas of Panama* Göteborg, 1947

Hoppál, M. (ed) *Shamanism in Eurasia* Herodot, Göttingen, 1984

Hoppál, M. and O. von Sadovszky (eds) *Shamanism Past and Present* 2 vols, Ethnographic Institute, Budapest and International Society for Trans-Oceanic Research, Los Angeles, 1989

Hoppál, M. and J. Pentikäinen (eds) *Northern Religions and Shamanism* Akadémiai Kiadó, Budapest and Finnish Literature Society, Helsinki, 1992

Hoppál, M and K Howard (eds) *Shamans and Cultures* Akadémiai Kiadó, Budapest and International Society for Trans-Oceanic Research, Los Angeles, 1993

Howell, S. *Society and Cosmos: Chewong of Peninsular Malaysia* University of Chicago Press, Chicago, 1989

Hultkrantz, Å. *The Religions of the American Indians*, University of California Press, Berkeley and Los Angeles, 1979

Hultkrantz, Å. *Shamanic Healing and Ritual Drama: Health and Medicine in Native North American Religious Traditions* Crossroad, New York, 1992

Humphrey, C. "Theories of North Asian Shamanism" in E. Gellner (ed) *Soviet and Western Anthropology* Duckworth, London, 1980

Humphrey, C. *Karl Marx Collective: Economy, Society and Religion in a Siberian Collective Farm* Cambridge University Press, Cambridge, 1983

Humphrey, C. *Journeys of the Mind: Sketches of Daur Shamanism* [provisional title] Oxford University Press, Oxford, in press

Jilek, W.G. *Indian Healing: Shamanic Ceremonialism in the Pacific Northwest Today* Hancock House, Surrey, British Columbia, 1982

Joralemon, D. "The Selling of the Shaman and the Problem of Informant Legitimacy" in *Journal of Anthropological Research* 46(2): 105–118, 1990

Kalweit, H. *Dream Time and Inner Space: the World of the Shaman* Shambala, Boston, 1984

Kapferer, B. *A Celebration of Demons: Exorcism and the Aesthetics of Healing in Sri Lanka* Indiana University Press, Boomington, 1983

Katz, R. *Boiling Energy: Community Healing among the Kalahari Kung* Harvard University Press, Cambridge, Mass, 1982

Kelly, K. *I See with Different Eyes* privately printed, Cambridge, UK, 1993

Kendall, L. *Shamans, Housewives, and Other Restless Spirits: Women in Korean Ritual Life* University of Hawaii Press, Honolulu, 1985

Kendall, L. *The Life and Hard Times of a Korean Shaman* University of Hawaii Press, Honolulu, 1988

Kendall, L. "Chini's Ambiguous Initiation" in Hoppál and Howard, 1993

Kendall, L. "Initiating Performance: the Story of Chini, a Korean Shaman" in C. Laderman and M. Roseman (eds) *The Performance of Healing* Routledge, New York, 1995

Kim, S.N. "Lamentations of the Dead: the Historical Imagery of Violence on Cheju Island, South Korea" in *Journal of Ritual Studies* 3/2: 251–85, 1989

Kleivan, I. and B. Sonne *Eskimos: Greenland and Canada* (Iconography of Religions series) Brill, Leiden, 1985

Ksenofontov, G.V. *Legendy i rasskazy o shamanakh u yakutov, buryat i tungusov* [*Legends and Tales about Shamans among the Yakut, Buryat and Tungus*] Izd. Bezbozhnik [Atheist Press], Moscow, 1930

Ksenofontov, G.V. *Shamanizm: izbrannyye trudy* [*Shamanism: Selected Works*] Sever-Yug, Yakutsk, 1992

La Barre, W. *The Ghost Dance: the Origins of Religion* Doubleday, Garden City, 1970

Lame Deer, J. and R. Erdoes *Lame Deer, Seeker of Visions* Simon and Schuster, New York, 1972

Langdon, E.J.M.L. and G. Baer *Portals of Power: Shamanism in South America* University of New Mexico Press, Albuquerque, 1992

Larsen, S. *The Shaman's Doorway: Opening Imagination to Power and Myth* Harper and Row, New York, 1976

Lévi-Strauss, C. *Structural Anthropology* Basic Books, New York, 1963

Lewis, I.M. *Religion in Context* Cambridge University Press, Cambridge, 1986

Lewis, I.M. *Ecstatic Religion: a Study of Shamanism and Spirit Possession* Routledge, London and New York, 1989

Lewis-Williams, J.D. and T.A. Dowson "The Signs of All Times: Entoptic Phenomena in Upper Palaeolithic Art" in *Current Anthropology* 29(2): 201–45, 1988

Lommel, A. *Shamanism: the Beginning of Art* McGraw Hill, New York [reviewed in *Current Anthropology* 39–48, 1970]

Lowenstein, T. *Eskimo Poems from Canada and Greenland* Allison and Busby, London, 1973

Lowenstein, T. *The Things That Were Said of Them: Shaman Stories and Oral Histories of the Tikigaq People Told by Asatchaq* University of California Press, Berkeley, 1992

Lowenstein, T. *Ancient Land, Sacred Whale: the Inuit Hunt and its Rituals* Bloomsbury, London, 1993

Luna, L.E. *Vegetalismo: Shamanism Among the Mestizo Population of the Peruvian Amazon* Almqvist and Wiksell, Stockholm, 1986

Luna, L.E. and P. Amaringo *Ayahuasca Visions: the Religious Iconography of a Peruvian Shaman* North Atlantic Books, Berkeley, 1991

Matthews, J. *Taliesin: Shamanism and the Bardic Mysteries in Britain and Ireland* Aquarian Press, London, 1991

Merkur, D. *Becoming Half-Hidden: Shamanism and Initiation among the Inuit* Almqvist and Wiksell, Stockholm, 1985

Merkur, D. *Powers Which We Do Not Know: the Gods and Spirits of the Inuit* University of Idaho Press, Moscow, Idaho, 1991

Michaelk, H.N. *Studies in Siberian Shamanism* University of Toronto Press, Toronto, 1963

Mumford, S.R. *Himalayan Dialogue: Tibetan Lamas and Gurung Shamans* University of Wisconsin Press, Madison, 1989

Myerhoff, B. *Peyote Hunt* Cornell University Press, Ithaca, New York, 1974

Neher, A. "A Physiological Explanation of Unusual Behaviour in Ceremonies Involving Drums" in *Human Biology* 34: 151–60, 1962

Nicholson, S. (ed) *Shamanism: an Expanded View of Reality* Theosophical Publishing House, Wheaton, Illinois, 1987

Noll, R. "Shamanism and Schizophrenia: a State Specific Approach to the 'Schizophrenia Metaphor' of Shamanic States" in *American*

Ethnologist 10: 443–61, 1983

Nuttall, M. *Arctic Homeland: Kinship, Community and Development in Northwest Greenland* University of Toronto Press, Toronto, 1992

Peters, L.G. *Ecstasy and Healing in Nepal: an Ethnopsychiatric Study of Tamang Shamanism* Undena, Malibu, 1982

Peters, L.G. and D. Price-Williams "Towards an Experiential Analysis of Shamanism" in *American Ethnologist* 7: 398–418, 1980

Popov, A.A. "Tavgiytsy [The Tavgy]" in *Trudy Instituta Antropologii i Etnografii* vol. 1, pt 5, Moscow and Leningrad, 1936

Popov, A.A. "Polucheniye Shamanskogo Dara [The Acquisition of the Shamanic Gift]" in *Trudy Instituta Etnografii AN SSSR* vol. II, Leningrad, 1947

Radin, P. "The Autobiography of a Winnebago Indian" in *University of California Publications in American Archaeology and Ethnology* vol. 16, 1920

Radin, P. *The Road of Life and Death* Pantheon, New York, 1945

Rasmussen, K. *The Intellectual Culture of the Iglulik Eskimos* Gyldendalske, Copenhagen, 1929

Reichel-Dolmatoff, G. *Amazonian Cosmos: the Sexual and Religious Symbolism of the Tukano Indians* University of Chicago Press, Chicago, 1971

Reichel-Dolmatoff, G. *The Shaman and the Jaguar: a Study of Narcotic Drugs among the Indians of Colombia* Temple University Press, Philadephia, 1975

Reichel-Dolmatoff, G. *Beyond the Milky Way: Hallucinatory Imagery of the Tukano Indians* University of California, Los Angeles, 1978

Ring, K. *Heading Towards Omega: in Search of the Meaning of the Near Death Experience* William Morrow, New York, 1984

Ripinsky-Naxon, M. *The Nature of Shamanism: Substance and Function of a Religious Metaphor* SUNY Press, Albany, 1993

Roseman, M. *Healing Sounds from the Malaysian Rainforest: Temiar Music and Medicine* University of California Press, Berkeley, 1991

Rouget, G. *Music and Trance* Chicago University Press, Chicago, 1985

Samuels, A. et al *A Critical Dictionary of Jungian Analysis* Routledge, London and New York 1986

Schultes, R.E. *The Healing Forest: Medicinal and Toxic Plants of the Northwest Amazon* Portland, Oregon, 1990

Schultes, R.E. and A. Hofmann *Plants of the Gods: Origins of Hallucinogenic Use* Hutchinson, London, 1979

Shaman: an International Journal for Shamanistic Research [Szeged, Hungary]

Sherzer, J. *Kuna Ways of Speaking: an Ethnographic Perspective* University of Texas Press, Austin, 1983

Shirokogoroff, S.M. *The Psychomental Complex of the Tungus* Kegan Paul, London, 1935

Shternberg, L.Ya *Pervobytnaya religiya v svete etnografii* [*Primordial Religion in the Light of Anthropology*] Institute of Northern Peoples, Leningrad, 1936. ("Shamanism and Religious Election" portion translated in S. and E. Dunn (eds) *Introduction to Soviet Ethnology* vol 1, Highgate Road Social Science Research Station, Berkeley)

Siikala, A-L *The Rite Technique of the Siberian Shaman,* Academia Scientiarum Fennica, Helsinki, 1978

Siikala, A.-L. and M. Hoppál *Studies on Shamanism* Finnish Anthropological Society, Helsinki and Akadémiai Kiadó, Budapest, 1992

Silverman, J. "Shamanism and Acute Schizophrenia" in *American Anthropologist* 69: 21–31, 1967

Steward, J. (ed) *The Handbook of South American Indians* 7 vols, Cooper Square, New York, 1963

Sturtevant, W.C. (ed) *The Handbook of North American Indians* 15 vols (not yet complete), Smithsonian Institution, Washington, 1978–

Suzuki, S. *Zen Mind, Beginner's Mind: Informal Talks on Zen Meditation and Practice* Weatherhill, New York and Tokyo, 1970

Taussig, M. *Shamanism, Colonialism and the Wild Man: a Study in Terror and Healing* University of Chicago Press, Chicago, 1987

Thomas, N. and C. Humphrey (eds) *Shamanism, History and the State* University of Michigan Press, Ann Arbor, 1994

Tsing, A.L. *In the Realm of the Diamond Queen* Princeton University Press, Princeton, 1993

Vitebsky, P. "Some Medieval European Views of Mongolian Shamanism" in *Journal of the Anglo-Mongolian Society* [Cambridge], 1(1): 24–42, 1974

Vitebsky, P. "Landscape and Self-Determination
    among the Eveny: the Political Environment
    of Siberian Reindeer Herders Today" in E.
    Croll and D. Parkin (eds) *Bush Base, Forest
    Farm: Culture, Environment and Development*
    Routledge, London, 1992
Vitebsky, P. *Dialogues with the Dead: the
    Discussion of Mortality among the Sora of
    Eastern India* Cambridge University Press,
    Cambridge, 1993
Vitebsky, P. "Deforestation and the Changing
    Spiritual Environment of the Sora" in R.
    Grove (ed) *Essays in the Environmental
    History of South and Southeast Asia* Oxford
    University Press, Delhi, 1995a
Vitebsky, P. "From Cosmology to
    Environmentalism: Shamanism as Local
    Knowledge in a Global Setting" in R.Fardon
    (ed) *Counterworks* Routledge, London, 1995b
Vitebsky, P. *The New Shamans: Psyche and
    Environment in an Age of Questing*
    [provisional title] Viking Penguin, New York,
    forthcoming
Walsh, R.N. *The Spirit of Shamanism* Tarcher,
    Los Angeles, 1990
Wasson, R.G. et al *Maria Sabina and her Mazatec
    Velada* Harcourt Brace Jovanovich, New
    York, 1974
Wauchope, R. (ed) *The Handbook of Middle
    American Indians* 16 vols plus later
    supplements, University of Texas, Austin,
    1964–76
Williams, W.L. *The Spirit and the Flesh: Sexual
    Diversity in American Indian Culture* Beacon,
    Boston, 1986

Index

X

Photo Credits

Abbreviations
B bottom; **C** centre; **T** top; **L** left; **R** right
DBP Duncan Baird Publishers
NY New York

1 Department of Indian Affairs, Canada/ Akpaliak, Manasie; 2 Michael Oppitz; 6/7 Greenland National Museum; 6T DBP/Strat Mastoris; 6B DBP/Strat Mastoris; 7B DBP/Strat Mastoris; 8/9 Edouard Luna/Pablo Amarigo; 10 DBP from *The New Mongolia* 1934, Forbath and Geleta; 10/11 Werner Forman Archive/Museum of British Columbia; 11 National Museum of Denmark; 12/13 Edouard Luna/Pablo Amarigo; 12 National Museum of Denmark; 13 Buffalo Bill Historical Center; 14 Museum of Mankind, British Museum; 15 from a painting by Elizabeth Goodall, courtesy of the National Museums and Monuments, Harare; 16 Jean-Pierre Chaumeuil; 17 Piers Vitebsky; 18 Department of Indian Affairs/Noah, William; 19 Josiane Cauquelin; 20/21 Fergus Bowes-Lyon; 22 DBP/Strat Mastoris; 23T DBP/Strat Mastoris; 23B DBP/ Strat Mastoris; 23C Robert Harding Picture Library/Heller; 24T Edouard Luna/Pablo Amarigo; 24B Benedicte Brac de la Perrière; 25T Museum of Mankind, British Museum; 25B Panos Pictures/French; 26/27 Hutchison Library/ Dodwell; 28T from a painting by Elizabeth Goodall, courtesy of the National Museums and Monuments, Harare; 29 from *Studies on shamanism* Siikala and Hoppál; 29B Jean Loup-Charmet; 30T Werner Forman Archive/Field Museum, Chicago; 30/31 DBP from *Aboriginal Siberia* Czaplcicka; 32B Werner Forman Archive/ Museum of Mankind; 32T Peter Furst; 32C Peter Furst; 33 Piers Vitebsky; 34 Piers Vitebsky; 35 American Museum of Natural History; 36/7 Carole Pegg; 36C Carole Pegg; 36B Carole Pegg; 37T Aspect/Carmichael; 37B Carole Pegg; 38 Josiane Cauquelin; 39R Laurel Kendall; 39L Hutchison Library/Dodwell; 40 Piers Vitebsky; 41T Rex Features; 41C Hutchison Library/Tann; 41B Piers Vitebsky; 43 National Museum of Art, Washington/Art Resource, NY; 45T Werner Forman Archive/Buffalo Bill Museum; 45B Werner Forman Archive/Field Museum, Chicago; 46B DBP from *Los mitos de creación y de destrucción del mundo* C. Nimuenajo; 46T Hutchison Picture Library/von Puttkamer; 46/47 Peter Gorman/Flores; 47T Peter Furst; 48T Panos Pictures/McDonald; 49T Hutchison Library/ Moser; 49C Peter Furst; 49B Peter Furst; 50 Robert Harding Library/Pinson; 51T Bridgeman Art Library, Christie's; 51B DBP from *Bushman Art – Rock Paintings of South West Africa* Hugo Obermair, Herbert Kuhn; 52/3 Michael Oppitz; 54 V.N. Basilov; 55 Michael Oppitz; 56T Jean-Pierre Chaumeuil; 56B Laurel Kendall; 57T Piers Vitebsky; 57B American Musuem of Natural History; 58 Josaine Cauquelin; 59 Edouard Luna/ Pablo Amarigo; 60 Werner Forman Archive/Field Museum, Chicago; 61 painting by Timofei Stepanov; 62 Michael Oppitz; 63T National Museum of Denmark; 63B Piers Vitebsky; 64T Hutchison Library/von Puttkamer; 64B Piers Vitebsky; 65T Jane Monnig Atkinson; 65B Richard Katz; 66T Werner Forman Archive/ Buffalo Bill Museum; 66B Werner Forman Archive/National Museum, Denmark; 67T Department of Indian Affairs, Canada/ Alikatuktuk, Ananarsie; 67B Department of Indian Affairs, Canada/Saila, Pauta; 68T Bryan & Cherry Alexander; 68C Werner Forman Archive/ Museum für Volkerkunde; 68B Peter Gorman/ Flores; 69T Nebraska Historical Society; 70B Werner Forman Archive/Museum für Volkerkunde; 71B DBP/Strat Mastoris; 71T Ferens Art Gallery, Hull City Museums; 72T Piers Vitebsky; 72B American Museum of Natural History; 74B Greenland National Museum; 75 Edouard Luna/Pablo Amarigo; 76T from *Monkey Subdues White Bone Demon*, Liaoning Publishing House; 77T DBP/Strat Mastoris; 77B Josaine Cauquelin; 76B Science Fiction Monthly/Josh Kirby; 77C American Museum of Natural History; 78T Laurel Kendall; 78B Piers Vitebsky; 79B Hutchison Library/ McIntyre; 79T Edouard Luna/Pablo Amarigo; 81B Michael Oppitz; 81TR Robert Harding Picture Library/Pinson; 81C Anthrophoto/ Richard Lee; 82TL Werner Forman Archive/ Provincial Museum of British Columbia; 82TC Werner Forman Archive/Provincial Museum of British Columbia; 82TR Werner Forman Archive/ Provincial Museum of British Columbia; 83B DBP/Strat Mastoris; 83T American Museum of Natural History; 84BL American Museum of Natural History; 84BR DBP/Strat Mastoris; 84TL Werner Forman Archive/Collection of Mr & Mrs Putnam; 84TR Werner Forman Archive/ Collection of Mr & Mrs Putnam; 85C Robert Harding Picture Library/Pinson; 85TL Natural History Picture Agency/Heuclin; 85BR Peter Gorman/Flores; 85TR Robert Harding Picture

Library/Pinson; **85BL** Hutchison Library/
McIntyre; **86B** Suttons Seeds; **86BR** Peter
Gorman/Flores; **86TL** Peter Gorman/Flores; **87**
Harvard Botanical Library, Courtesy of Mrs
Masha Arnold; **88B** Derek Fordham/Arctic
Camera; **88C** Bryan & Cherry Alexander; **89**
Judith Pettigrew; **88T** from a drawing by Karale,
1920; **90T** Mary Evans Picture Library; **90B** Peter
Furst; **91** American Museum of Natural History;
92T Edouard Luna/Pablo Amarigo; **92B**
Department of Indian Affairs, Canada/Mark
Uqouyuittuq; **93** Southwest Museum, Los
Angeles; **94TL** Kishor Tamu (Gurung); **94B**
Kishor Tamu (Gurung); **94TR** Judith Pettigrew;
95B Michael Oppitz; **95T** Werner Forman
Archive/Terry P Will Collection, Alaska; **96/7**
Piers Vitebsky; **98B** Michael Oppitz; **98T** Werner
Forman Archive/B. Colman; **99T** The Bridgeman
Art Library, Prado Museum, Madrid; **100T** Jean-
Pierre Chaumeuil; **100C** Jean-Pierre Chaumeuil;
100B Jean-Pierre Chaumeuil; **101** Piers Vitebsky;
102B Anthrophoto/Irwin DeVore; **102T** Piers
Vitebsky; **104T** Michael Oppitz; **104B** Werner
Forman Archive/Private Collection; **104C** Carole
Pegg; **105** Josiane Cauquelin; **106BR** Werner
Forman Archive/Glenbow Museum; **106L**
Museum of Mankind London, British Museum;
106/107 Bryan and Cherry Alexander; **107C**
Survival Anglia/Foott; **107B** Mark Nuttall; **108B**
Jean-Pierre Chaumeuil; **108T** from *Maps and
Dreams* Hugh Brodie; **109** from *Beyond the Milky
Way* Gerardo Reichel-Dolmatoff, University of
California Press; **110/111** Piers Vitebsky; **111B**
Werner Forman Archive/William Channing
Collection; **111** Jane Monnig Atkinson; **112/113**
from *Religiya Evenkov* AF Asinimov; **113T** from a
drawing by Gert Lyberth, 1915; **114/115** Edouard
Luna/Pablo Amarigo; **115B** Piers Vitebsky; **116T**
Hulton Deutsch; **116B** Popperfoto; **117** Piers
Vitebsky; **118T** Werner Forman Archive/private
collection, New York; **119B** Laurel Kendall; **119T**
Judith Pettigrew; **120T** Werner Forman Archive/
Provincial Museum, Britsh Columbia; **120** Werner
Forman Archive/Field Museum, Chicago; **121**
DBP/Ulrike Preuss, Courtesy of Kaos Theatre;
122 Michael Oppitz; **123TR** Hutchison Library/
McIntyre; **123TL** Laurel Kendall; **125T**
Etnografiske Museet, Oslo; **126T** Werner Forman
Archive/Field Museum of Natural History,
Chicago; **127** DBP from *Mythology of all races*
vol iv Finno Ugric Siberia, 1927; **128/129** Private
Collection; **130B** from a drawing by Karale, 1920;
130T Werner Forman Archive/Private Collection;
131T from Gilij 1781 1193 Bodleian 233E45O
reproduced with permission of the Bodleian
Library, Oxford; **131B** Novosti Press Agency;

132B Robert Harding Picture Library; **132T** Piers
Vitebsky; **133B** Hutchison Library/Cliverd; **133T**
Rex Features; **134** Piers Vitebsky; **135** Aspect/
Carmichael; **136T** Piers Vitebsky; **136B** The
Hutchison Library; **138BL** from *Intellectual
Culture of the Hudson Bay Eskimos* Knud
Rasmussen; **138B** Private Collection; **139T** from
Intellectual Culture of the Hudson Bay Eskimos
Knud Rasmussen; **139B** Private Collection; **140**
Private Collection; **141** Private Collection; **142B**
American Museum of Natural History; **142T** Jane
Monnig Atkinson; **143T** Piers Vitebsky; **143B**
Piers Vitebsky; **144** Piers Vitebsky; **146** Charles
Macdonald; **147** Private Collection; **148T**
National Museum of Denmark; **149T** Robert
Harding Picture Library/Michael Jenner; **150**
Lazslo Kunkovacs; **151B** Department of Indian
Affairs, Lucy Ottochie; **152** Lazslo Kunkovacs; **153** Rex
Features; **154** from *Monkey Subdues the White
Bone Demon* Liaoning Art Publishing House; **155**
Piers Vitebsky; **156** Piers Vitebsky; **157T** Edouard
Luna/Pablo Amarigo; **157B** Images Colour
Library; **159** DBP from *Mu-Iglala, or the way of
Muu* Holmer and Wassén; **160** Michael Oppitz;
163 Timofei Stepanov; **165** Ohio Historical
Society; **167** painting by Jessie Oonark, Winnipeg
Art Gallery purchased through a grant from
Imperial Oil Limited, photo Sheila Spence

AUTHOR'S ACKNOWLEDGMENTS

I owe a great debt to the many shamans and their clients
who have helped me over the years, to the scholars whose
works have taught me and to the many institutions which
have enabled me to travel. Jonathan Horwitz, Laurel
Kendall, Mark Nuttall and Judith Pettigrew kindly com-
mented on the manuscript but should not be blamed for
any faults which remain. I dedicate this book to my wife
Sally in gratitude for her support and understanding.

DISCLAIMER

This book includes scientific, historical and cultural
information concerning plants which are or have been of
importance to many societies. Ingestion of some plants or
plant products may be highly dangerous. Shamans use
such plants and substances only after strict and arduous
training. Neither the author nor the publishers take
responsibility for the consequences of any reader
ingesting plants or plant products which have been
mentioned in the book.